15.6.06

Emerging Evangelism

Emerging Evangelism

JOHN FINNEY

DARTON·LONGMAN+TODD

First published in 2004 by
Darton, Longman and Todd Ltd
1 Spencer Court
140–142 Wandsworth High Street
London SW18 4JJ

ISBN 0–232–52496–3

A catalogue record for this book is available from the British Library.

Unless otherwise stated, the Scripture quotations in this publication
are taken from the New Revised Standard Version © 1989, 1995.
Division of Christian Education of the National Council of the
Churches of Christ in the United States of America.

Phototypeset in 9.5/13.25pt Palatino by Intype Libra Ltd
Printed and bound in Great Britain by
Page Bros, Norwich, Norfolk

CONTENTS

INTRODUCTION

I never went to church as a child. I was never sent to Sunday School. I suddenly encountered God when I was seventeen, and he became electrifyingly real to me. Possibly because of this I have always been fascinated by the boundary between faith and unfaith. What happens when people cross this boundary? What helps or hinders this process? Where is the Church in all this and what theology lies behind it all? What does the surrounding culture have to say?

For more than thirty years I have wrestled with the issues surrounding the Church and its mission. As vicar of three parishes, then as diocesan Adviser in Evangelism and national Officer for the Decade of Evangelism I had these matters thrust before me. Subsequently as bishop in an area with one of the lowest churchgoing rates in the country I had to help to lead the Church in its mission. I have been much involved in the writing and promotion of nurture courses, and have co-authored both *Saints Alive!* and the *Emmaus* course.

The debate about the right way to evangelise is of vital importance for the future of the Church in the Western world and perhaps its very existence in any coherent form. I hope this book will encourage this discussion and open new possibilities. It is not merely a critique of modern evangelism, though this is where we ought to start, but also a practical book which makes suggestions for the future – and it even includes outlines of three possible evangelistic sermons!

In this book we shall be looking at evangelism, its history and its character, and I try to summarise the fascinating results of recent statistical research. But we shall look more deeply than that.

1

The **methods** whereby we convey the gospel are important, but more significant still is the **content** of the gospel we transmit and the **shape** of the church which expresses it. I shall argue that all too often we have so 'cabined, cribbed, confined' the gospel message and restricted what we mean by 'church' that we have sold people short and diminished the majesty of what God has revealed to us in Christ. J.B. Phillips' book was famously entitled *Your God is Too Small:*[1] I shall argue that we have made the gospel too small. Moreover, too often we have not only diminished it, we have controlled it and made it a commodity. It should be the vehicle of the Holy Spirit who is like the clear wind that sweeps in from the wild places. Too often we have marketed it like a commercial product.

By this I do not mean there is anything wrong with the gospel but I wonder if our interpretation of it has been too often formed in our own image, making it shallow when it should be deep, and narrow when it should be broad.

The first two chapters introduce the current position by looking at the present situation of the Church, the ongoing discussion about the nature of evangelism and my suggestions about the fully orbed and unifying biblical model which we should use. Chapter 3 examines the context in which we evangelise, and Chapters 4 and 5 give an overview of the history of evangelism and especially the radical and often unnoticed change which has occurred in the UK during the very recent past. Chapter 6 suggests that we need to learn from the ministry of Paul recorded in the New Testament to see how he dealt with pagan surroundings, and how we too should broaden our evangelistic message. The next three chapters look at the different models of church community which are emerging, the leadership needed to surmount the obstacles of modern society and what 'clicks' with post-modernist people. The final chapter points to two particular needs – learning and holiness – and sums up the book: **the Church and its gospel needs to be broader and deeper.**

Down the years we receive far more from others than we think. Some people I have been able to acknowledge, while other names have long disappeared into the murk of memory. For all the half-remembered words and chance remarks which started me thinking, and above all the experiences which proved significant, I give you all thanks: forgive me that I cannot thank each of you.

Above all my thanks to Almighty God and the boundless, wondrous message which he has entrusted to frail men and women.

CHAPTER 1

Looking at the Realities

Where we are now

In Lancashire I once saw a small public garden. In it was a plaque put there by the local authority: 'Site of a Methodist chapel, built 1846, enlarged 1906, demolished 1988'. As I sat in the garden I thought of all the effort which must have been put into the chapel over the years – the raising of the money, the building of the chapel – and then the excitement as the building became so crowded that they needed to enlarge it. And then the heart-breaking sight of the bulldozers. Extinction can happen.

Decline in church attendance is taking place across almost all of the Christian denominations (with a few exceptions which we shall try to learn from later). Visits to Holland and Germany have shown me that this is not confined to the United Kingdom. In Holland churchgoing is still a little higher than in the UK but the rate of decline is so fast that it will soon be less. In Germany churchgoing is already less than in the UK and sinking. Nor is it better in 'Catholic' Europe, where Italy, Spain, Bavaria and elsewhere are recording aging, declining congregations and a desperate shortage of priests.[1] In Canada and Australasia the same depressing decline is taking place. Until recently the US seemed to be the great exception – an industrialised, developed nation with a high rate of churchgoing. At the time of the American Revolution in 1776 there were barely 5 per cent of Americans in church on a Sunday: attendance steadily climbed to over 40 per cent in the 1980s. Now, however, there are sad signs that it may be following the pattern of the rest of the Western world, though from a much higher baseline.[2]

But if we look at almost any other part of the world we see a different story. Asia, Africa, South America show the Church growing or at worst holding its own. Yet these are often places of difficulty and persecution. From our depressing Western scene what can we learn from them? I knew a missionary from Britain, who, it was said at her funeral, 'was born to be made head girl': she had a powerful personality. But her ministry was transformed when she had the humility to kneel in front of the Rwandan Christians she had come to teach and say, 'Please lay hands on me that I may have what you have'. Perhaps Western Christianity needs to say the same to the Christians in the two-thirds world and receive through them.

But is churchgoing important? The yardstick used by most denominations is Usual Sunday Attendance. It has many short-comings – what about those who come on weekdays? are children included? what about those who come regularly but once a fort-night? Nevertheless, it does represent something important for it indicates the degree of belonging. And the most persuasive recent sociological work shows that the great majority of people who come to faith belong *before* they believe. Robin Gill has argued cogently that a decline in church attendance comes first and as a consequence there is a decline in faith.[3]

Jesus began his ministry with the call, 'repent and believe the good news' (Mark 1:15). Repentance (*metanoia*) begins with accu-racy – coolly facing the reality of our own sin, or the sin of the Church or the sin of the world. To help us to do this I shall not flinch from statistics, for good statistics can give us a useful snap-shot of a situation. Fear of figures leads to fantasy. An all-too-familiar figure is the minister who always maintained his church was growing, but whose congregation was smaller when he left than when he came. To deny reality is to live in a land of delusion.

Money makes most churches face up to reality. In few churches now are there any longer the cushioning reserves in the accounts, the 'income from other sources' which prevented congregations realising the true cost of running their churches, the bountiful budgets which enabled work to be done without researching how effective it was. There is no doubt that the Church of England began to take evangelism seriously when the loss of money in the early 1990s meant that it had to look at the primary question, 'What is this Church here for?' Martyn Atkins does not speak only of the Methodist Church when he says, 'We will not see how far down the road to death we are until that comforting, blinding money is gone'.[4]

But merely facing up to the actual situation is not enough: indeed, it can be unduly depressing, for we are people of faith. We also face reality by seeing things through the eyes of God: 'The fear of the Lord is the beginning of wisdom'.[5] I hope this book will be a spiritual journey as well as a practical exercise. That is why the first chapter is an examination of the gospel from God's viewpoint, in which we look at the place of the Trinity in the *evangel* and the different aspects of evangelism which are portrayed in the Bible. What is God like? If we do not begin with God, then we are simply picking up the latest wheeze, the most fashionable bandwagon or the last thing we read in a book or heard at a conference.

Next, we need to look at the backcloth against which our evangelism takes place and examine the context of our present culture, with its strange mix of modernism and post-modernism. We then seek to learn from the past (in Chapters 4 and 5) as we look at the history of evangelism in the past couple of centuries and see why the gospel had become packaged and miniaturised – but also to look at the considerable change in the thinking behind evangelism and its practice that has happened in some countries in the past twenty years or so.

But there are two introductory questions which need to be answered to clear the ground:

A. What *exactly* is evangelism? *and*
B. Why religion at all?

A. What *exactly* is evangelism?

Evangelism is a word which provokes strong reactions. Some good Christian folk see it as something to be avoided at all costs: others see it as absolutely essential. Why the emotional sensitivity?

In the 1980s and early 1990s I was supposed to help people to start doing some intelligent evangelising. My job titles showed this – 'Adviser in Evangelism'; 'Officer for the Decade of Evangelism'. I was asked over and over again: 'You have come to tell us about evangelism, but what *is* it?' It is a fair question.

Too many hours of my life have been spent sitting in rooms agonising over definitions of the word.[6] Out of hundreds of possibilities I find most workable the one given by William Abraham: 'that set of intentional activities which is governed by the goal of initiating people into the Kingdom of God'.[7] But that does not end the discussion.

Ten Christian leaders are sitting round a table. They want to work together to evangelise their town. They want to deal with the practicalities of the mission but have first to think about what each means by evangelism. One is a Baptist, one is a Roman Catholic priest, and the rest are either Anglicans or from other strands of Christendom. They do not know each other well, and so are rather defensive. There are six areas around which debate rages:

1. Are we going to use the words 'evangelism' and 'evangelists' at all? Wouldn't it be better to use other words such as 'evangelisation' or 'missioners'?
There is no doubt that the very word 'evangelism' sets many people's teeth on edge. It is seen as a good word which has been spoilt by being associated with 'mass evangelism' – the great rally, the massed choirs, the simple (simplistic?) message, the big preacher. As Michael Green says: 'Evangelism does not enjoy a good press. It conjures up lurid, imaginative and often negative impressions of strident, perspiring preachers, of smooth-talking evangelists, of strange characters at street corners urging the passers-by to repent and meet their God.'[8] Or as *Good News People* says: 'The evangelist nearly always gets a bad press. In the

media he (it usually is a he) is depicted as loud and insensitive, overintense, humourless and manipulative. It is the image of the pushy salesman.'[9] Not surprisingly people think twice about inviting an evangelist to come to their town. Too easily the caricature of the evangelist comes to the fore, and the antics of Elmer Gantry fester at the back of people's minds.

By the 1980s the word 'evangelist' had become narrowed in the minds of many, both within and outside the Church, to those who practise 'stadium' evangelism. It was sometimes even called 'crusade' evangelism, with all the anti-Muslim overtones of that word. Many saw it as 'aggressive', 'unthinking', 'fundamentalist', 'crude'. The thought of being associated with what they consider a form of Christian imperialism is anathema to several in our group of ten, and they see 'evangelism' as a word to be avoided.

Some in the group, therefore, suggest the more general word 'mission', much beloved in ecumenical documents (and even more difficult to define with exactness). Others want to retain the sharper edge of the word 'evangelism', fearing that there would not be a definite 'gospel message' if it is not used. The Roman Catholic priest favours the word 'evangelisation', used in many papal encyclicals, as avoiding the worst overtones of 'evangelism' (which for him has strong political overtones because of the situation in South America).

The discussion about words goes round and round in the group until eventually they decide that 'evangelism' is acceptable, provided that it is understood to be wider than a certain style of evangelism. In fact, in the last fifteen years, evangelism has become a much more acceptable word, not least because stadium evangelism is much less in evidence. Nevertheless, around the table the word still arouses negative feelings.

2. Are we to use the word 'proclamation'?
Three or four in the room see evangelism as just 'preaching the gospel'. They know the truth; others don't and they need to hear it. It is a matter of verbal communication from those who know

about God to those who do not. The ignorant are to be informed of the way of salvation so that they may walk along it and be saved. For them the word 'proclamation' enshrines their favourite place of communication – the pulpit.

But for others in the group such 'take it or leave it' preaching is manipulative and lacking respect for those who are being preached at. This division represents a basic difference of viewpoint that we shall come across frequently. On the one hand, there are those who see evangelism in term of confrontation – one person facing another and telling that individual to desert his or her former allegiance and change sides. On the other, there are those who see evangelism in terms of two people walking side by side and talking together. For the former 'proclamation' represents all that they are trying to do. For the latter it represents all that they dislike.

There is no doubt that the word 'proclamation' is biblical, and that conveying the good news by preaching has been common since the earliest days of the Church. However, the nub of the argument is whether that is seen as one method among many or *the* main way in which people are brought to God through Christ. For some preaching is seen as almost the only way by which people are brought to faith – pastoral care, friendship, social work are only means by which people are enticed to come 'under the Word of God' and hear and believe.

To the surprise of some in the group the Methodist minister, known to be an evangelical, wants the mission *not* to concentrate on preaching. He says that people react differently these days, and they need opportunities to put their point of view and discuss the momentous decision they are being asked to make. What is more, he says, preaching by itself has been shown not to work very well: research in the 1990s revealed that only a comparatively small number of people come to faith through preaching. If the Church had to rely on preaching for bringing people to faith it would be highly ineffective.

The group reach a compromise – there is to be *some* preaching, but many other things as well.

3. Do we see evangelism just as the conveying of a formula?

Later in this book we shall examine historically how certain formulae of salvation came into being with each generation seeing its formula as the only 'real' gospel. For many, the kernel of evangelism requires the person being evangelised to assent to certain propositions, with 'Do you admit you are a sinner?' usually being the first. Some of those around the table have in their minds a 'golden road' to becoming a Christian: it is deeply personal, and absolutely vital for true 'conversion'. It is likely that they themselves had found Christ through the same formula.

For others around the table this is hopelessly individualistic. It forgets the social context from which the potential convert comes and the difference which being a Christian should mean to society around. But when challenged by the first group as to 'What is *their* gospel?', they find it difficult to reply because they think the Christian faith is much more than having a form of words to be easily formulated. If pushed they will mumble 'the Creed' or 'the promises of baptism', but they are uneasy about any set formula.

In practice, in any such discussion I have found it useful to help people to enunciate what they mean by 'gospel': very often Christians use different words to describe the same thing, and explanation is all that is required. However, sometimes there are differences of great complexity which need to be faced. Here we are at the heart of the Christian message and, if these issues are not in the open, progress is likely to be slight. I hope the second half of the next chapter will make a contribution to both explaining these differences and bringing Christians with these differing viewpoints to a unity of spirit.

4. What shall we do about the Church?

This is a real battleground. Some around the table want to have as little to do with the Church as possible when they are defining evangelism. They see the Church as regrettable and off-putting: 'People want Jesus, not a whole lot of Churchianity'. Others say that the gospel comes from the Church and even that the Church is part of the gospel. Whether they like it or not, the inescapable truth is that, when someone becomes a Christian, they become part of the Church. The first group see the Church as Christ's 'leprous bride' which is just a distraction, while the others see the Church, at least in theory, as potentially being 'without spot or wrinkle'.[10] For them it is ridiculous to talk about Christ without also talking about the Body of Christ.

This discussion has moved on in recent years. On the whole Christians of different traditions are agreed that the Church cannot be left out of the equation. The message, however biblical, is inevitably conveyed by those who are members of the Church.

5. Where shall we put the other bits of the gospel – justice, care for the poor, Christian standards and so on?
This is an argument about priorities. On the one hand, there are those who say, 'We have to put the horse before the cart – make sure people are Christians and then all the other things will follow.' Others respond, 'People need to know that the gospel is more than just a conversion experience – the gospel has repercussions which have to be worked out.'

This debate often degenerates into biblical texts being used like hand grenades. One side will toss over John 3:16, 'You must be born again' (NIV), only to have Mark 10:25 lobbed back, 'It is easier for a camel to go through the eye of a needle than for someone who is rich to enter the kingdom of God.' The first antagonist then hurls over Mark 1:14, 'The kingdom of God has come near; repent and believe in the good news', and is met by Matthew 25:34, 'Come, you that are blessed by my Father, inherit the kingdom prepared for you from the foundation of the world: for I was hungry and you gave me food . . .'. The discussion then goes on to the epistles which are ransacked for texts, until the Bible becomes no more than an arms dump from which to gather ammunition.

6. How should we ask people to respond to the gospel?
Some round the table want definite 'conversions' – we shall be selling people short if we do not give them a chance to say 'Yes' to

Jesus. Others are not so sure. They speak of the need to respect their integrity, of the fact that not everybody comes quite so openly to faith (citing Nicodemus coming by night in John 3) and the research which shows that most people experience faith as a journey which can take some time. Some around the table will therefore be looking for a mission in which there are definite opportunities for people to express their newfound commitment to Christ – by coming to the front for counselling at a meeting. Two of the ministers have charismatic leanings and want opportunities for people to 'receive ministry' and the laying on of hands. The Roman Catholic priest may want to mark this moment by asking people to make their confession for the first time.

The discussion lasts far beyond the time allotted but slowly, through talking and praying, hard positions soften and suspicion diminishes. In the end they agree: the gospel will go forth in their town.

B. Why religion at all?

L'église – NON; l'institution – NON; Dieu – OUI.

David Brown, a church planter in France, sums up the current dilemma of the Church.[11] The Church is bewildered by a population which sees it as having very little to do with spirituality. For centuries it has been taken for granted that

> spirituality = something to do with God = something which the church is expert at.

Whether it was prayer or worship or being in tune with creation, a Godward focus was taken as obvious. Indeed, this was true even of atheists – old-fashioned atheists assumed that because they did not believe in God they had no spiritual life.

Since the bulk of people then thought that the Church had a monopoly on the subject of 'God' and explaining his ways to the world and in teaching about 'the spiritual life', they turned to it to deal with that side of their personality. But now the Church sees the world turning its back and looking elsewhere for guidance. Its influence ebbs away. Even amidst the religiosity of Northern Ireland David Bruce can speak about the 'shortening shadow of the steeple'.

It is not as though people no longer have spiritual longings: in Peter Berger's words, people are still as 'furiously religious as ever'.[12] Every magazine is full of spiritual advice, and wave after wave of new spiritualities wash over the Western world. Indeed, one of the accepted factors about them is their transience – they rise to a peak buoyed on a froth of publicity, and then fade away. For a time nobody who aspired to be at the height of fashion could fail to adjust their life and their furniture to take account of Feng Shui which, they were told, 'can help prevent or solve over 90% of life issues, including adultery, financial entrapment, strange, conventionally untreatable illnesses, depression and repetitive relationship collapse'.[13] It appears as though the more recent a spirituality is, the more powerful it seems to be. One is reminded of the hucksters in the marketplace who sold snake oil which they claimed could cure everything from bunions to a broken leg.

People now engage in what has been called a 'mosaic' approach to life in which they inhabit many different worlds and have many different attitudes in each. As Bob Dylan said in 1997:

> I don't think I'm tangible to myself. I mean, I think one thing today and I think another thing tomorrow. I change during the course of a day. I wake and I'm one person, and when I go to sleep I know for certain I'm somebody else. I don't know who I am most of the time. It doesn't even matter to me.[14]

It can all degenerate into a frantic search for personal happiness. The 'me-generation', which is desirous of clothes only if they have a designer label, has bypassed a Church which seems deeply unfashionable.

The result of self-gratification is not necessarily beneficial. The Old Testament prophets pointed out that wealth does not lead to either godliness or personal happiness. As Lord Layard, the Labour Government's employment guru, said:

> As a society we are richer than ever, living healthier, longer lives, with more political and social freedoms and less fear of war, famine or natural disaster. Yet we are no happier than previous generations, with rates of depression, suicide, alcoholism and criminal delinquency all rising.

In the Middle Ages the different faiths – whether the Christian faith or any other – were never referred to as 'religions'. It was only in the seventeenth century, with the dawning Enlightenment and the encounter with non-European people who seemed to believe in different gods, that the word began to be used to describe particular systems of belief and ritual. With the growth of sociology religion began to be increasingly seen as a subject of study and comparison, though it is clear that when the early sociologists wrote they were primarily studying the Christian faith.

'Religion' gets a bad press from those outside the Church. It is popularly defined in two ways. On one hand, it is seen as 'institutional', burdened with organisations and the lust for power, and cold-hearted in dealing with the needs of individuals. On the other hand, it is regarded as a motivating force for violence and division – hence there are 'Islamic terrorists', 'Hindu militants', 'Catholic (or Protestant) gunmen', 'Jewish fundamentalists'.[15] On either understanding it means that religion gets cast into the fiery furnace which modern people reserve for antiquated and dangerous ideas. Externally a religion is seen as yet another authoritarian institution, and philosophically as a meta-narrative to be thrown away along with all nostrums which seek to explain the world.

It is not only from those outside the Church that 'religion' gets a bad press. In 1927 Dietrich Bonhoeffer spoke of 'religionless Christianity'. In *The Communion of Saints* he declared that the Church was not 'an association of religiously interested people', for Christianity was 'not religion, but revelation, not a religious community, but the church. That is what the reality of Jesus Christ means'.[16] Karl Barth (1886–1968) protested that God could not be known by human endeavour, for only by God's own revelation could he be known. Religion, and that included Christianity, was an idol to be rejected.

In 1966 William Hamilton took Bonhoeffer's ideas further:

> The God of religion, solving otherwise insoluble prob-
> lems, meeting otherwise unmeetable needs, is
> impossible and unnecessary. Thus man cannot be
> said to need God at all, God is not necessary to
> man . . . The plea for a religionless Christianity is
> thus a plea to give up all claims for the necessity of
> religion generally. Christianity – as would be true of
> any religion and any irreligion – is not necessary. It is
> merely one of the possibilities available to man in a
> competitive and pluralistic spiritual situation today.[17]

But is 'religionless Christianity' possible? It sounds so plausible, even desirable – let us cut away the dead weight of what the Christian faith has become through history and return to the simplicity of a man or woman before their Creator – assuming there is a Creator. Delete the Church and the stigma of history and be free!

Unfortunately it is not so easy. In saying to the disciples 'Follow me', Christ was not only inviting them to share one-to-one spiritual intimacy. Implicit in that invitation is the command: 'Join them.' The disciples had to become part of that quarrelsome, bewildered group of men and women who were his followers. Like it or not the gathering of the believers was an essential part of being a Christian. Indeed, 'religionless Christianity' is yet another symptom of that Western individualism which shrinks from the collective.

In 1969 Ninian Smart suggested that a religion is 'a six dimensional organism, typically containing doctrine, myths, ethical teachings, rituals, and social institutions, and animated by religious experiences of various kinds'.[18] It can hardly be denied that on that definition Christianity is a religion. Nor can it be claimed that the whole of Christianity is a perversion of what Christ left us, for so many of those elements go back to the Saviour himself who left us teaching about his Father and how we should live our lives in community under his lordship.

From the point of view of presenting Christ to others today the link between Christianity and religion may be a disadvantage to evangelism, but we do ourselves no favours by pretending that it is other than it is. The gospel is about the coming of a particular person into the world, what he revealed to us about God and the impact that should have upon our lives. In the eighteenth century Lessing spoke about the 'ugly ditch' which has opened up between the world of the Bible and his day – and it has certainly not narrowed since then. To build a highway across that gap so that many thousands may rejoice in Jesus Christ is our duty and our joy.

In this book we shall try to build a few girders into that structure.

CHAPTER 2

'Not In Word Only . . .'

Conversion

> Jesus has forgiven all my sins and I need not walk in
> fear again. Everything has a purpose in God's plan.
> Through God I will live forever. God is my Father and
> my friend. He is always with me. I am not alone any
> more. He loves me.[1]

Joanna's sense of release, security and hope could be echoed by a
million others who have been 'converted'. They know that their
lives will never be the same and they feel more secure as people
and closer to God.

The spiritual and psychological impact of conversion cannot be
denied. Pinning it down by a definition is far more difficult.
Defining 'evangelism' is difficult enough, but 'conversion' is even
more difficult because it is dealing with the complexities and
individualities of human beings. Lewis Rambo describes the
concept in words which echo both the New Testament and the
experience of many who would say they have been 'born again':

> Conversion is paradoxical. It is exclusive. It is inclusive. It
> destroys and it saves. Conversion is sudden and it is
> gradual. It is created totally by the action of God, and it
> is created totally by the action of humans. Conversion is
> personal and communal, private and public. It is passive
> and active. It is a retreat from the world. It is a resolution
> of conflict and an empowerment to go into the world
> and to confront, if not create, conflict. Conversion is an
> event and a process. It is an ending and a beginning.

It is final and open-ended. Conversion leaves us
devastated – and transformed.[2]

If it is to be real to the Bible and to what people actually experience when they undergo a religious conversion, any definition
cannot but have the wide, wide limits set by Rambo. Is it sudden
– or is it gradual? It is both. Is it the end of a journey or its
beginning? It is both. Does it bring peace or a sword? It brings
both. Vast controversies have rolled across theological battlefields
– Calvinists would say that, 'Conversion is wholly the work of a
sovereign God', while Arminians would claim that human free
will also has a part to play.

But is this all-embracing, all-transforming encounter which
Rambo describes the only way in which God can be experienced?
Is there a less high-octane, less passionate, possibly more frequent
form of conversion? What about those who would call themselves
Christian but would reject the title of 'born again'? For them their
faith is more diffuse, less obvious, more private. G.W. Allport
drew a distinction between 'intrinsic' faith, which was the all-
demanding conversion we have just described, and 'extrinsic'
faith, which he described as 'strictly utilitarian: useful for the self
in granting safety, social standing, solace and endorsement for
one's chosen way of life'.[3] The reality of this kind of extrinsic faith
is obvious to anyone who has looked at an average congregation.
There are those who keep their faith in a box, to be produced on
Sunday but apparently having little impact on their life from
Monday to Saturday. But is Allport's description of such a faith as
'utilitarian' unduly dismissive? All pastors come across those who
cannot put their faith into words, but for whom it is the bedrock of
their life; who pray simply, but sincerely; who worship traditionally but wholeheartedly; who may not witness verbally but whose
lives shine.

It is all too easy for those who have a vivid intrinsic faith to look
down on the apparently plodding faith of the extrinsics – indeed,
to wonder if they are really Christians at all. Yet sometimes the
tortoise has greater staying power than the hare: pastorally one

finds that the faith of the intrinsics can be rooted in shallow ground and shrivels in adversity, while the extrinsics have a greater ability to withstand the shocks of life.

Sudden or gradual?
Down the years the experience of conversion has been looked at in various ways. Some have seen it as an *event* as sudden as throwing the switch of a floodlight – instantaneous, overwhelming. Others have seen it as a *process* like the rising of the sun: the sky changes from black to grey, and then come the first pink clouds until gradually the sun begins a new day. At what time during dawn do we actually experience sunrise? The important thing is that the sun has come.

However, this may be too simplistic. Before the floodlight was lit there had to be preparation. When those who have had a sudden conversion are asked in detail about their experience, they can often perceive events which led up to what seemed at the time to be an explosion of faith. Scot McKnight, in his book *Turning to Jesus*, even argues from his examination of both the New Testament and modern experience that conversion is always a process – but that sometimes it is a very short process![4] Even a closer look at Saul, whose experience on the Damascus road is seen as the archetypal sudden conversion, suggests it was perhaps less instant than first appears: he had witnessed Stephen's martyrdom – and what was happening three days later when Ananias laid his hands upon Saul 'so that you may regain your sight and *be filled with the Holy Spirit'*?[5]

On the other hand, those who see the gradual dawning of the day are faced by the meteorologist who says that 'sunrise is at 06.31'. Whether or not there is a moment of acceptance by God we do not know, and we would be foolish to second-guess him. Churches are fond of head hunting, seeking to add to the numbers of the 'converted'. King David got into trouble when he tried to count his people, and we are wise not to seek to know the unknowable.

In the New Testament there are two symbolic roads. Travellers to Damascus experience something unpredictable, sudden, almost irresistible. Those who go to Emmaus encounter the Stranger without a name, and explore, question, listen, take their time.[6]

Another way of interpreting the New Testament is to distinguish between Paul and John. Because of his own personal experience it is not surprising that Paul stresses that conversion is an event. It is a passing from darkness to light, from one kingdom to another, a time when 'everything has become new!' (2 Cor. 5:17). For John it is less clear-cut. As John Bowen from Wycliffe College in Toronto puts it:

> When John speaks of someone as 'believing' he does not mean a sudden, once-for-all translation from darkness to light, as Paul might characterise it. For John, belief means rather that someone is engaged in a movement away from darkness and towards light. They are in what we might call an evangelistic process. 'Believing' in John is simply an indication of direction.[7]

In John's Gospel people often show the direction they are pointing by asking a question, and these questions often sound sceptical and uncertain, even apparently hostile. Further, in John these people are not seen just as those who are on the way to faith but are already counted as disciples. It is not for nothing that John is the only Gospel which tells us anything personal about Thomas. His aggressive expostulation to Christ in 11:16, his angry cry of bewilderment in 14:5 and his refusal to believe in the resurrection without direct proof in chapter 20 are all typical. Yet it is Thomas who gives also the most wholehearted expression of faith in all the Gospels – 'My Lord and my God!' (20:28).

My own research showed that 69 per cent of adults experienced their coming to faith as a gradual process while 31 per cent could give a date on which they experienced conversion.[8] It is not a matter of either event or process. *Different people experience God in different ways and any sensitive evangelism must allow for both types of experience.*

Transmission of the gospel

One of the oddities of the letters of St Paul is how he, one of the greatest evangelists the world has ever known, speaks so little about evangelism. Even when writing to churches he had founded himself, he says very little about his own work of evangelism amongst them: there are few nostalgic reminiscences. It makes the few references there are particularly valuable in helping us to discern how Paul went about doing the work of an evangelist. Apart from a few brief and uninformative references there are only three which enlarge on his evangelistic ministry. They are set out here in the probable order they were written:

1. 1 Thessalonians 1:5: *'our message of the gospel came to you not in word only, but also in power and in the Holy Spirit and with full conviction . . .'*
Paul's evangelism was to do with spoken words, but that was certainly not all. It is difficult to be sure exactly what events he is referring to when he talks of 'power . . . Holy Spirit . . . conviction', but it can hardly be less than the charismatic overtones which we see so often in Acts where 'signs and wonders' were so frequently witnessed in association with evangelism. His meaning would, of course, have been immediately apparent to those in Thessalonica for they had personally experienced what he was talking about. It shows us that a 'word only' evangelism is not enough: there has to be the expectation and the experience of something which is other than words. Later in this chapter we shall examine the different New Testament words associated with evangelism and we shall find that the word *mysterion* is used to describe this non-verbal evangelism.

2. 1 Corinthians 2:1–4: *'When I came to you, brothers and sister, I did not come proclaiming the mystery of God to you in lofty words or wisdom. For I decided to know nothing among you except Jesus Christ and him crucified. And I came to you in weakness and in fear and in much trembling. My speech and my proclamation were not with plausible*

words of wisdom but with a demonstration of the Spirit and of power, so that your faith might rest not on human wisdom but on the power of God.'

In this emotionally charged passage Paul deliberately plays down the power of his preaching so that the faith of the Corinthians might be seen to rest on the power of God through 'a demonstration of the Spirit'. In the scheme of the epistle, knowing that he was writing to a church where he was being heavily criticised, he wanted to emphasise that it was God's power which had brought them to faith, not the impact of his personality. In many ways it reinforces the Thessalonian passage. Paul is once again saying that a 'word only' evangelism is only partial evangelism. Once again there are charismatic overtones in the 'demonstration' of the Spirit – and once again our curiosity about what exactly happened is not satisfied! The Greek word for 'demonstration' is that used by Greek philosophers as a sort of QED for an argument, so Paul is suggesting that what happened was a certain proof to the Corinthians of the reality of God.

3. Romans 15:18–20: *'I will not venture to speak of anything except what Christ has accomplished through me to win obedience from the Gentiles, by word and deed, by the power of signs and wonders, by the power of the Spirit of God so that . . . I have fully proclaimed the good news of Christ. Thus I make it my ambition to proclaim the good news, not where Christ has been already named . . .'*

In this passage he is explaining his evangelistic strategy to a church with which he has had no personal contact: he seeks to proclaim the gospel in unevangelised Gentile areas. He also tells the church at Rome something about his methods: we have a reference to 'deed' as well as word. As in the Thessalonians passage, he cites the 'signs and wonders' and the 'power of the Spirit of God' which accompany his preaching. The gifts of the Spirit are in evidence alongside his proclamation.

The similarities between these three passages, written at different stages of Paul's ministry, are extraordinary. In all three the *'word'* is mentioned; clearly the spoken word was an important part of Paul's evangelism. But in every passage there is also the word *'power'*, and in each case it is closely linked with the person of the Holy Spirit. Indeed, in the Corinthians passage he says that the word is less significant than the power of the Holy Spirit. That Paul expected his evangelism to have both components cannot be denied.

If our evangelism is to echo that of Paul it must have both the word and the power of the Holy Spirit. The significance of the non-verbal is also brought to the fore when we look at the three words which are used in the New Testament to describe the process of evangelism. Two of them may be familiar: the third is seldom examined in this context.

Kerugma . . . evangelion . . . mysterion

These three Greek words describe different aspects of the gospel. Each can be taken as representing a different approach to evangelism. (Whether the way they have come to be employed accurately reflects the strict meaning of the words as they are used in the New Testament is another matter, but they are certainly useful handles to examine the subject further.) I will retain the Greek words for, as we shall see, no single English word can do justice to the nuances of their full meaning in their original language.

Kerugma – the content of the gospel

The background to this word is a herald (*keryx*) and what he does. In the Greek world the herald could be someone as exalted as a messenger of the gods or as matter of fact as the local town crier who announced next week's market. But he did not only give information about forthcoming events: in a period before newspapers and television, he was also the person from whom most people heard news from afar – of a battle won or lost, or of a royal birth or death. What sort of person the herald was mattered little – what was important was the content of his message. Above all he had to be accurate in his transmission of the message: at the Olympic games there were competitions for heralds at which they were tested for the loudness of their voice and their precision in passing on a message.

To pass on information means to educate. Hence evangelism which concentrates on passing on the *kerugma* will inevitably have a strong educational bias. The gospel is seen as facts (and hopefully an encircling ethos) to be conveyed, especially to the young. Such evangelism will, therefore, have considerable emphasis on schools, whether state or private, and it is because of this that many schools in the UK have a religious foundation. Anglican and Roman Catholic churches put much effort and money into providing a Christian education for a sizeable proportion of the community.[9] In the UK there are 7000 church schools – a third of the total. While it is often assumed that the church contribution to education is declining, in reality the Church of England alone has in recent years established more than thirty new secondary schools and many primary schools are either being planned or built, and the present government is urging the establishment of yet more.

But educational evangelism is not confined to schools. Churches which use this method look to having a good Christian education, through training systems for adults and a staged series of programmes for young people through Sunday Schools, young people's groups and the like. Indeed, worship services themselves are seen as having an educational content, particularly through the sermon, but also through the liturgy and music.

The fact that all churches have such an educational process (or wish that they did!) reminds us that when we talk about evangelism we are not locked into one style of evangelism. While it is true that, because of their large number of schools, this seems to be primarily an Anglican and Roman Catholic methodology with their talk of 'Christian formation' by a catechetical process, it is by no means confined to them. It can be labelled as a typically 'Catholic' approach, but it is certainly not limited to those who would be happy with that label.

It is always wise to see what are the possible *negative* results of any form of evangelism. I would suggest that concentration on the *kerugma* tends:

1. *to promote a hierarchical view of the Church.* If there are the taught, then there are also the teachers, and they become the authority figures dispensing truth. Where there is authority there is also the exercise of power. This is carried to an extreme in the Roman Catholic Church where the teaching authority (the 'magisterium') is focused on one man working through a myriad of sub-teachers. As the official Catechism says, 'The Roman Pontiff, head of the college of bishops, enjoys this infallibility, when, as supreme pastor and teacher of all the faithful . . . he proclaims by a definite act a doctrine pertaining to faith or morals' (891). But this claim to authoritative teaching is by no means confined to Roman Catholicism. There are many Protestant or Pentecostal popes: wherever one person (or a small group) sets him or herself up as the fountainhead of authority over others there will be a hierarchy.

2. *to demand a meticulously accurate definition of the faith.* The faith needs an authoritative textbook from which it can be taught. Some have looked to the Bible, others to papal encyclicals, or to a particular reading of 'tradition', to the Heidelberg Catechism, or to 'sound' writings by Aquinas, by Calvin, or whoever. The use of quotations from the authoritative written text, of course, encourages those who are taught to believe that a replication of that text is more important than understanding what it is trying to convey.

3. *to externalise the faith.* Saying the correct words becomes more important than having a relationship with God and witnessing to the world. Time and again the Church has gone down this path. Protestants and Catholics have demanded doctrinally flawless

statements to be made by new members when they are only trying to express in their own stammering way the faith that is within them. Emphasis on education means an emphasis on exams, and getting it right.

4. *to be more left brain than right.* Rationality is seen as more important than intuition, intellectuality as more important than the emotions. The result can be a desiccated bigot rather than a man or woman of faith.

Evangelion – the gospel and its proclamation

The *evangelion* is news – and that is not all, it is good news. The verb which goes with it (*evangelizomai*) means to 'proclaim the good news'. Among the Greeks it was a technical term for the proclamation of a victory: when an *evangelion* was announced, the messenger who brought the news was ritually crowned with a laurel wreath – and given a reward.[10] The word has a note of urgency – the sprightly messenger was honoured while those who were dilatory were punished.

In this form of evangelism the proclamation is all important: the passing on of the Word is all.[11] As John Stott says, 'Evangelism is the announcement of the good news, irrespective of the results'.[12] The word is proclaimed and a response is awaited. Often allied to it is a belief that the time is short before Christ returns so there is not a moment to be lost.[13] Proclamation is to be done by all means possible, but especially through preaching. Therefore, the task of evangelism is to make sure that the Word is heard by as many people as possible. This has practical consequences, for money is not put into the lengthy process of building schools and educating the young, but into 'mass evangelism', into the use of radio, TV and the Internet, and into training evangelists who will go out and preach the gospel.

So much had evangelism become associated with this style of preaching that when the Anglican Bishops in 1988 called for a 'Decade of Evangelism' it was misunderstood as being a call for only that style of evangelism. As an Officer for the Decade I found time and again that in people's minds evangelism = Billy Graham. Not surprisingly the thought of ten years of non-stop mass evangelism was not appealing.

And what are the negative elements of this form of evangelism?

1. *It can diminish the importance of the Church as an element within the gospel.* Indeed, it can diminish the fellowship of believers to an unfortunate appendage which is best ignored. Because there is so much concentration upon the need of the individual to come to God, the corporate nature of faith is ignored.

2. Because the emphasis is so much upon ensuring that as many people as possible hear the Word *there can be an excessive concern with numbers.*

3. *In some of its forms it can become manipulative* (as we shall see in Chapter 3). It is all too easy to treat everyone the same, so that the journey to God becomes a series of hoops through which it is expected that everyone should jump.

4. *It can lead to a Lowest Common Denominator gospel* by which the basic message which is applicable to the largest number becomes the norm. Just as over-emphasis on the *kerugma* can over-intellectualise the gospel, so exclusive stress on the *evangelion* can lead to an over-simplification of the gospel. *Metanoia* is no longer the full-orbed repentance of the New Testament but becomes merely being sorry for our sins. Conversion becomes no more than a psychological process with religious overtones. In particular, it can so overemphasise the second person of the Trinity that the invitation to follow God becomes a call to 'invite Jesus into your heart'.[14]

However, both *kerugma* and *evangelion* have the same short-coming: they are dependent upon *words*. Whether they are words taught or words preached, they produce a forest of verbiage. And we have found that Paul saw his evangelism as having another ingredient – the power of the Holy Spirit. Evangelism which is dependent only upon education and/or preaching is seriously deficient in terms of the New Testament.

St Francis said that 'it is no use walking anywhere to preach unless our walking is our preaching'. If we rely on words it opens us to the all too close-to-the-bone comment of E.M. Forster, 'Poor, talkative, Christianity'.

Fortunately for our wellbeing the New Testament provides us with another Greek word, which may not be as frequently cited in theology books as *kerugma* and *evangelion*, but which expresses the transmission of the gospel by other means.

Mysterion – the mystery of the gospel

Mysterion is used twenty-eight times in the New Testament. It is sometimes mistranslated as 'secret', as though God had had something tucked away which he divulged to the apostles and so now it is no longer a secret. That makes God's purposes sound like a detective novel where the murderer is discovered in the last chapter: in that case the problem is solved and is no longer a mystery. *Mysterion* is a much deeper word than just describing a secret which suddenly pops out of a box. Rather, as Brien Kostenberger and Peter Andreas say, it describes the gospel as a divine mystery which 'is revealed, is being revealed and is to be revealed . . . the broad sweep of God's salvation-historical plan is in view when the term "mystery" is used'.[15] It is revealed in Christ and it continues to be revealed to the human soul as the light of God touches each one of us and even the history of our planet. But that is not the end: there is also an eschatological element in which the mystery will not be fully revealed until the End. As Moltmann says:

> *Mysterion* is an apocalyptic term for the future already resolved on by God, for the end of history . . . Its revelation in history has the character of a veiled announcement of a promise of the future, and of anticipation. Its revelation at the end of history takes place when it is openly put into effect. Jesus is the revelation of the eschatological mystery

of God through his mission, his death and his resurrection from the dead.[16]

I confess I reach this scriptural term connected with evangelism with some relief. The thought of evangelism being no more than a torrent of words battering the world is sad. It makes it seem as though God's mission is dependent upon us getting a verbal formula exactly right and then teaching it or preaching it to as many people as possible. If I may say so reverently, 'Thank God evangelism does not depend upon our teaching and preaching'. Words-only evangelism can be mechanical, unimaginative, even unspiritual. If we rightly want more evangelism, does this just mean that more words have to come avalanching forth? Is evangelism just a beehive of activism? *Mysterion* suggests there is more to it than that.

All real evangelists, however persuasive their teaching or their preaching, know well that there is another ingredient besides their words. Why one person who hears the Word is deeply influenced and brought to faith while the person beside them walks away unmoved is impossible to say. The mystery is there, deep within the human soul.

We need this element of mystery. Romans 8:15–16 tells of that deepest of places within us where our spirit and God's Spirit intertwine and bring forth the great shout of recognition and realisation, 'Abba – Father'. How and why this happens is impossible to say for it is the subterranean work of the Spirit of God. In the New Testament *mysterion* is a rich word:

(a) *it usually describes God's work of communication* – the *mysterion* is 'taught', 'told', 'shown', 'proclaimed' . . . 'revealed' by him.[17] Paul describes how he received the *mysterion* from God by 'revelation' (Eph. 3:3).

(b) *it is the work of the Holy Spirit.* 'It has now been revealed to his holy apostles and prophets by the Spirit' (Eph. 3:5). It brings to our minds the reliance upon the Holy Spirit and power which we have seen earlier in Paul's descriptions of his own ministry.

(c) *there is an element of choice* – in the famous passage
   in the Gospel where Jesus talks about the purpose of
   his parables there are some who hear 'the *mysterion* of
   the kingdom of God' while others do not (Mark 4:11
   and parallel passages).

(d) *it was essentially hidden in the past* (Col. 1:26; Eph. 3:9)
   but now the sun has begun to rise as part of God's
   overall plan becomes apparent: it was 'decreed before
   the ages for our glory' (1 Cor. 2:7).

(e) *it was not just an experience of God: it had content* –
   Paul speaks of the good news for the Gentiles and our
   personal resurrection in Christ and in 1 Timothy 3:16
   the mystery is expressed in the form of a creed:

> He was revealed in flesh,
> vindicated in spirit,
> seen by angels,
> proclaimed among the Gentiles,
> believed in throughout the world,
> taken up in glory.

Graham Tomlin is right when he says the word *mysterion* 'seems
to express something very important to Paul'.[18] After all we are
talking about a relationship – and a relationship which is dependent upon words is thin indeed. Friendship is real when deep
speaks to deep in human life – by things unsaid, by those shared
experiences which become 'sacramental signs', by the glance of
mutual understanding.

So it was when Christ came. The birth of yet another baby and
the all-too-common sight of someone crucified become shot
through with *mysterion* as they display the wonder of the incarnation and atonement. In the Eastern Church in particular these
great facts are still referred to as 'the holy mysteries', as also is the
Eucharist which portrays them. Indeed, the thinking and practice
of the Orthodox Churches have retained the sense of the *mysterion*
more fully than the coolly intellectual Western Churches, whether

Roman Catholic or Protestant, which demand a rationale for all things. Gregory of Nazianzus (329–89) spoke for the best of Orthodoxy when he said that a true theologian was not someone who could give a completely logical account of Christian doctrine but someone who 'assembles more of Truth's image and shadow'. It is instructive to note that the Orthodox Churches in Western Europe are almost the only denominations which are growing numerically: mystery attracts.

The Enlightenment curbed the human sense of wonder. Creation became subject to our wills and minds. It resulted in a world which was 'closed, essentially complete and unchanging . . . simple and shallow, and fundamentally unmysterious – a rigidly programmed machine'.[19] But the human spirit demands more than explanations. We need new worlds to explore, both in the physical universe around us and in the inner realm of the spirit.

In today's world Christians can try to explain too much. The modern world would kneel beside us if we bowed in humility before the truth as it is in God, and acknowledged that we do not know everything. It is certainly more appealing than when we profess to have the answer to all things in heaven and earth. As *Q Magazine* said in writing of the work of John Tavener, the Orthodox composer, 'Christianity's talent for shooting itself in the foot is nowhere better displayed than in its recent drive to de-mystify itself. After all, who goes to church to get reasonable? Mystery is precisely what used to draw the crowds; no wonder the gates are down.'

There was in the person of Jesus himself something of *mysterion*. It both puzzled and upset the disciples: he was like themselves in so many ways, but at a deeper level he was different. Any presentation of the gospel which does not have this sense of apartness denies him. As William Abraham says, 'there is an element of ineradicable mystery in the gospel and in the doctrines that have been inspired by it'.[20]

But *mysterion* does not answer all our problems. As before, we have to look at the possible negatives of an evangelism built upon only one outlook. If we concentrate on *mysterion* alone:

1. *People can be led into a maze without a map.* People can search and search but never find unless they have the objective guides provided by the Bible and the help of other Christians.

2. *It can lead into an over-fascination with the unusual.* 'Signs' is a word often used in John's Gospel to designate the healings and wondrous events which accompanied the inrush of the gospel. But they are just that: signs which point towards God. Someone on a journey would be unwise to stop to admire the signpost without going on the path it indicates.

3. *It can be too experiential and dependent upon the intuitive.* Just as *kerugma* and *evangelion* can be too logical and left brain, so *mysterion* can be too dependent upon right-brain thinking.

4. *It can lose its links with the historical facts of the life of Jesus* and the traditional content of the faith. The New Testament rightly links *mysterion* with the facts of faith: as Jesus said it is the '*mysterion* of the kingdom'. Faith without a link with the historic faith is a jellyfish faith floating wherever the currents take us.

Conclusion and challenge

It seems from our examination that no one of the three great New Testament words which speak of the faith and its transmission is enough in itself. Taken separately, each has serious problems and several negatives. Nor are we just talking about theory: there are too many existing situations which concentrate almost exclusively upon one method, and consequently swallow up much Christian energy and money. It is not enough to depend entirely upon any one of them.

We can take it a stage further: I believe it contains the kernel of an exceedingly important truth. There may be an element of caricature and overemphasis, but these distinctions are still very much with us.

Those who concentrate on *kerugma* teach often about the work of *God as Father* and Creator. Further, they often centre their teaching on the incarnation and the presence of God in his world, so the hub of their faith is often seen as the stable at Bethlehem when 'the Word became flesh and lived among us' (John 1:14). They hope that the response to their teaching will be seen in a life which is increasingly lived worshipping the incarnate God within the Church and mirrored in the world. They expect conversion to be gradual.

Those who stress the need for *evangelion* centre their preaching on *Jesus*. His passion and crucifixion is their focus, and older evangelicals still talk of 'preaching the cross' as shorthand for delivering a gospel sermon. The doctrine of the atonement is proclaimed again and again, often in its substitutionary form. For them the response to the preaching is some outward mark of repentance as the penitent comes beneath the shadow of the cross. They expect conversion to be sudden.

Those whose approach to the gospel is through *mysterion* rejoice in the work of the *Holy Spirit*. Their favourite passage is the sending of the Holy Spirit in Acts 2. They emphasise the great *ruach* of God which sweeps in from unknown places and disturbs and cleans. For them the response to the Spirit is seen in being ministered to by receiving the laying on of hands with prayer: sometimes outward manifestations of the work of the Holy Spirit, such as the gift of tongues, are expected to be manifested. Conversion to a life lived in the power of the Spirit may be either gradual or sudden.

But the three persons of the Trinity are a Unity. The life of Jesus is one – the birth at Bethlehem, the death at Golgotha and the sending of his Spirit are not to be separated. This suggests that it is only in the synergy of the Trinity and the whole life of the Christ that a fully formed evangelism can be found. To concentrate on only one element in evangelism is no more legitimate than to focus on only one Person of the Trinity or one part of the life of Christ. The Church, both internationally and locally, must express its evangelism in a threefold way.

We can take this a further and challenging step. Christians have always been prone to say that their particular outlook and methodology is right and all the others are wrong. Those who concentrate on teaching the faith may reject preaching as simplistic, while preachers cannot abide the intellectualism of the teachers. Both in their turn abhor the subjectivism of those who rely on human intuition: they try to shine the light of rationality upon the 'signs' and associate spiritual experiences with an excess of charismania.

In many ways *kerugma, evangelion* and *mysterion* represent the characteristics of the three great rivers of Christianity: Catholic, Protestant, Pentecostal.

The conclusion must be that if we need every person of the Trinity to have a full-orbed evangelism, then we cannot afford to concentrate on one aspect and reject the others. Long ago in 1952 Lesslie Newbigin wrote about the different outlooks of the three main strands of Christendom:

> . . . either we have to say that we are right and our fellow Christians in the other two strands have got it wrong, or we say that we have got it partly right and we ought to incorporate the other two strands into our thinking. The biblical evidence which supports all three strands suggests that the latter is right. This must be the centre of our ecumenical mission and may well lead the individual Christian into a pilgrimage into the spiritual riches of the strands with which he or she is unfamiliar.

More than forty years ago I read those words in Lesslie's book *The Household of God*[21] and they had a profound effect upon my spirituality and my outlook. As someone brought up as a good Protestant I began, cautiously at first, to explore the spirituality of both the Catholic and Pentecostal strands. I found riches I had never dreamed of.

The joining together of the three strands is no less important today. It takes the whole Church to evangelise the whole world. And in case we feel that it all depends on us we need to recall that we are undertaking the *missio dei* in company with the Triune God and that 'all mission and evangelism is follow-up work that comes after what God has already done in Jesus Christ'.[22] Jesus is the 'primal missionary'.

CHAPTER 3

What *Do* They Believe? Modernism and Post-modernism

The bizarre bird

A few years ago post-modernism burst upon the Christian world. There were endless conferences, books and discussions. Christians gasped, 'So this is the world we live in' and were mightily puzzled as to how they should cope with it.

Post-modernism is defined by the hyphen. If we are being accurate it is 'post-modernism', not 'postmodernism'. In other words it merely describes the sort of thinking which has come after modernism – it is not a coherent philosophy of its own.[1] It is as difficult to grasp as smoke and just as pervasive. It says that each of us forms our own way of thinking, based on our own experience of life. Thus it is sometimes referred to as an intellectual 'mosaic' where everyone gathers what pleases them in a pattern. But a mosaic is static: an alternative, and more dynamic, metaphor is that of a kaleidoscope, where the pattern is shaken from time to time and forms new patterns in response to outside forces. So right and wrong are outmoded: we can make up our own ethics and need no outside authority to impose anything on us. No Big Brother is accepted as the arbiter of all things, whether a politician, a scientist or a pope. There is an intense dislike of any scheme of thought, whether it is an 'ism' like communism or capitalism, or an 'ization' like globalization or Americanization. The same distaste also applies to any religious system of thought. Rigour is derided, whether of an exact science or a doctrinal system, so there is a doubt about all scientific 'progress' or indeed anything which seeks to explain everything, including all religions and all scientific 'world-views'.[2]

The Church generally only started to realise fully the significance of post-modernism in the 1980s. As Sweet says:

> Western Christianity went to sleep in a modern world governed by the gods of reason and observation. It is awakening to a post-modern world open to revelation and hungry for experience. Indeed, one of the last places post-moderns expect to be 'spiritual' is the church. In the midst of spiritual 'heating up' in the post-modern culture, the church is stuck in the modern freezer.[3]

As Christians became aware of this strange unexplored thinking they stood amazed: as Keats' 'stout Cortes' gazed at the new-found Pacific with a 'wild surmise', so they felt they had discovered a new ocean of thought. Some saw post-modernism as the latest work of the devil while others felt that they were liberated from the old, sterile arguments with modernism into a world which honoured spirituality and rejoiced in experience.

Now, some years later, we can take a more balanced view. The world has not completely gone touchy feely; not everything is swept into some misty New Age spirituality; there is such a thing as truth, though just saying 'It is true, because I say it's true' is not enough. We are finding that the modernity which stems from the Enlightenment has not completely vanished in a puff of smoke: it is still around and people still look for proof and argument and logic. But post-modernism is also with us in all its fuzzy splendour.

Today's culture is like a quaint bird. The left wing is still modernist – clear-cut, rational and suspicious of emotion. But the right wing is post-modernist and seeks to embrace the whole of human existence, not just the intellectual. The trouble is that this right wing believes in anything, but as soon as it does so, the scepticism inherent in the left wing immediately questions its validity.

As Michael Moynagh argues in *Changing World, Changing Church*,[4] we have different values in different places. In the workplace truth and accuracy do matter, teamwork is important, moral judgements have to be made and our outlook is largely modernist. But as soon as we leave the office or factory we become thoroughly post-modernist consumers where pleasure and appearance are all and our individual wellbeing is paramount. This leads to a 'double-mindedness', which the Epistle of James describes as inherently unstable,[5] and reflects a lack of integration within a fundamental part of our physical make-up since the left and right halves of our brain have the characteristics of these two wings. The tension, which has been so fruitful for the human race, for all great art and music comes from the intermixing of the two, can become corrosive. Possibly because there is no generally accepted social structure within which the two parts of our being can act in creative tension, the inherent division in the human make-up has become discordant rather than harmonious.

Nowhere is this more obvious than in the effects upon society. Bauman uses the vivid illustration of liquefaction: when an earthquake shakes previously solid ground it becomes a liquid with devastating results. When the framework of law and the common understandings of behaviour disappear, then society shudders and falls. In the name of the light of liberty we move into darkness.[6]

The two wings do not fit together very well and as a result modern culture shows every sign of flying around in circles. On the one hand, we accept the scientific and, on the other, we embrace the non-scientific: we accept nothing that cannot be proved, and yet are swept along by any gust of emotion.

Often this is a personal matter and our views are formed by an emotional reaction to a particular situation. The media know this well: a TV debate on euthanasia will nearly always be preceded by the graphic story of someone who suffered greatly before death. A subject, which above all needs to be discussed rationally, is thus trumped by an emotional card.

Nor is this just a matter of individual emotion. The national reaction in the UK to such events as the death of Diana, Princess of Wales, the proposal to put a few pence on petrol and the murder of Holly Wells and Jessica Chapman in Soham all show that the individualism fostered by modernism can be swept aside by a gale of post-modernist collective emotion.[7]

We Christians should not think we escape. We also are creatures of our age. We have the same two uncertain wings. Sometimes we try to believe that we are only carried along on the wings of the Spirit, but in reality we can no more escape the culture we live in than avoid the air we breathe. We too often react in exactly the same way as our neighbours, share their concerns and also have our thinking guided by the media. The mismatch between the two wings is shown in the fierce debates about doctrine and experience. Some Christians emphasise doctrinal truth above all else – either expressed as 'Catholic teaching' or 'biblical truth'. Others want to emphasise the senses and the free flow of the Holy Spirit as experienced through human beings. The first are the left-brain 'modernists' who desire certainty based on strict exegesis of the Bible or tradition. The second are the right-brain 'post-modernists' whose energies come from their experience of God. The gulf is wide – the modernists blame the post-modernists for woolly thinking and the latter accuse the former of a coldly intellectual approach to the faith without a real conversion of the heart. The current debate about the acceptance of practising homosexuals within the leadership of the Church shows this all too well.

Most Christians try clumsily to fly with both wings, but it is not easy, since the two cultural wings are themselves faulty. Hence we ourselves are often 'double-minded'.[8] Indeed, the discussion in James about 'faith' and 'works' is very relevant, for the mutual misunderstanding between orthodoxy ('right belief') and orthopraxis ('right action') runs deep in the Christian tradition. I myself, like many contemporary Christians, find it difficult to steer between those who cry, 'Doctrine is all-important or you will lose the faith', and those who say, 'Without a personal experience of God your faith is dead'. But it is a tension which has to be worked through if we are to engage with the modern world. Otherwise we retreat into a private world of prim intellectualism or an inward-looking coterie seeking the latest 'spiritual experience'.

The question 'Well, what do they believe?' is, therefore, not an easy one to answer. We are a double-minded generation. Contemporary men and women have a rational and modernist part of their mind which looks for proof, reasons and convincing argument. But at the same time there is the post-modernist segment open to many non-rational influences.

At its best it can be said that we are at last reacting as full human beings, not being ashamed of those parts of our humanity which are not explicable by reason. On the other it has to be said that these 'non-rational influences' can be benign or harmful. They range from a helpful emphasis on the importance of human relationships to the darker side of mass hysteria and fascination with the occult.

Secularisation

> Once upon a sociological time, the secular world-view was predicted to darken the sacred, ethics was foretold to cause the demise of religion, and the rise of science was prophesied to quench religious 'superstition'. The modern mind, so it was said, had little tolerance for rumours of angels.[9]

Margaret Poloma describes the course of human thought predicted by sociologists. It was expected that the steady advance of secularisation in human thinking and behaviour would continue until all past superstitions and ideologies had been gobbled up. It has not happened. Even though the Pope frequently blames 'secularisation' as the cause of many modern evils, it is doubtful if it can be blamed for church decline. Secularists are as bewildered as anyone by what is happening in the resurgence of religion around the world, often blaming the advent of post-modernism. For example, in 1971, in *Religion and the Decline of Magic*,[10] Keith Thomas looked back on the decline of belief in astrology and declared, 'the intellectual vitality the subject once possessed is gone for ever'. His description of the position thirty years ago is correct, but it is doubtful if astrology today has ever been more widespread, more sophisticated or more part of the culture of our times.

'I'm not religious but I definitely believe in something.' This comment from a sociological study shows why secularists are bemused. Modern men and women have not trooped to join the Rationalist Society: indeed, its very name has a musty Victorian air about it redolent of long-dead disputes. People may not know what their faith consists in but they certainly believe: it may be that because they no longer feel under any compulsion to adopt a particular religious stance they are more ready to explore and experiment. This is not confined to young people: 'The poverty of the rational, cognitive and scientific approaches to human existence that have emerged from the Enlightenment demand that this [spiritual] dimension of our lives is more thoroughly explored, and, as people age, this dimension grows in importance.'[11]

David Gill has done the Church great service in debunking the prevalent theory among sociologists of religion that secularisation is all-triumphant. This 'myth', as he calls it, is easily dismissed. For example, the middle classes who were the first to imbibe the values of secularisation are the last to be afflicted by church decline.[12] It is not enough for the Church to wring its hands and blame secularisation. As we shall see, the challenge may lie nearer home.

The place of the Church

Modernism has confronted the Church with many challenges over the past two hundred years. The Victorians agonised when they heard the 'long withdrawing roar' of religion,[13] saw the growth of Darwinism, the apparently all-conquering march of science and the secularisation of many institutions. More recently the ethical dilemmas created by discoveries in our genetic make-up have confronted the Church with endless dilemmas as we face the question 'What makes us human?' At the same time the self-indulgent but

insistent temptations of an ever-changing, vivid hedonism con-
stantly asking, 'What makes me happy?' can make the Church
seem grey and lifeless.

Post-modernism appears to offer a way out for, if all certainties
are gone, then with them go the certainties of science and the
awkward questions it poses. But, unfortunately, it is not only certainty which goes out of the window – truth is also jettisoned. And
Christians feel ill at ease when there is no foundation.

In the sky inhabited by the awkward two-winged bird the
Church has to learn how to soar. Over the past two hundred years
the Church has come to terms with modernism, adopted its hall-
marks, learnt to speak its language. It is true that the decline of
churchgoing has been allied with the rise of modernism, but we
have to be cautious about making too easy an equation between
the two. We find that the same is true of all mass movements
which are dependent upon regular attendance. Such bodies as
political parties, trade unions and the British Legion and many
youth organisations have also declined.[14]

The Church has tried to come to terms with modernism by
changing its organisation, its thinking and its practice.
Organisationally it has adopted the managerial stance of many
businesses: it has set objectives, streamlined middle-management,
introduced appraisal schemes, collected statistics. This was not
necessarily wrong, but it was certainly an imitation of the pattern
of secular business practice.[15]

Theologically there have been two attempts to come to terms
with modernism. Some attempted to 'make the faith acceptable to
modern man'. A tide of liberal thinking swept over theological
colleges and seduced many ministers: some denominations nearly
drowned in its waters. To be a scholar was admirable: to be an
evangelist was scorned. It is good to notice that the main intention
was missiological – to make the Christian faith seem amenable to
reason so that modern men and women could become Christians
without a leap into the dark of faith. However, all too often it
merely made impotent what is essentially a relationship with God
which is beyond human comprehension. To explain a mystery is to

lose its majesty. While there is certainly nothing wrong with apologetics (the New Testament is full of it), it should be a cool explanation of the gospel and its implications in all their fullness. It should not so dilute the gospel that it ceases to be good news.

Another response was fundamentalism, for it is also thoroughly modernist. The careful formulation of doctrine, the distrust of emotion and experience, the individualisation of our response to God and the apparently rational approach to the words of the Bible make the fundamentalist Churches children of the Enlightenment.

In its worship the changes of the twentieth century were manifold. All Churches produced different liturgies and different music to make the words more understandable to the congregation. In particular, in the Roman Catholic Church not merely the words of the liturgy were changed but the whole setting and conduct of the mass. Even non-liturgical churches changed their routine and the words they used. Again, the intention was missiological – so that those who were not brought up to sing the old hymns and mouth the traditional words could take a full part in the service. At times it has been very modernist in that it assumed that the words were all important for they appealed to the understanding. But good worship, of course, does not just appeal to the left side of the brain but to all of us. If this does not happen, then we cannot worship with all our heart and mind and soul. Again it must be said that this liturgical renewal is not wrong – even if at times it appeals too much to our brain and not enough to our heart. Attending a church service in any denomination in 2000 is almost certainly markedly different from what was happening in that church in 1900, and nearly all the changes have been in a modernist direction.

In short, the Churches made their accommodation with modernism. But we may be in danger of continuing to fight the battles of the last war, not grasping the possibilities of the future. As William Storrar says of the Presbyterian Church of Scotland: 'The Kirk is intellectually and institutionally a declining *modern* organization in an increasingly *post-modern* society'.[16] In other words, the Church is flying too much with its left wing and so is spiralling downwards. As modernism declines, a modernist Church declines with it. In particular danger are those Protestant Churches, like the Presbyterian Church of Scotland, which lay great stress on the proclamation of the Word, and so make their appeal primarily to human rationality. If the modernist slant of so many churches is not balanced by the non-intellectual approach of post-modernity, their appeal will continue to dwindle. As Storrar also says:

> The Church is more than a social institution caught up in the sweep of historical change. It is also the Body of Christ called to faithfulness and continuing reformation within the loving purposes of God for the world. The Kirk has been too preoccupied with the fruitless search for modern methods to reverse institutional decline and insufficiently committed to theological reflection on the nature and mission of the church in a post-modern world.[17]

The New Age Movement

New Age spirituality has moved from the extreme edge of public acceptability to the centre of many people's thinking. When it began to emerge in the 1970s it was thought to be a hangover from the hippie age and would soon wilt along with flower power. On the contrary, in the post-modernist compost it has flourished and multiplied exceedingly. To confirm the pervasiveness of New Age thinking one merely needs to glance at the 'Body, Mind and Spirit' shelves in a bookshop, or look at the many 'lifestyle' magazines or become aware of the crystals, motifs and charms with which people adorn themselves.

In her attack on post-modernism, Edith Wyschogrod says,

> . . . in unburdening itself of a nomological structure [i.e. ethical standards] it has thrown away morality, in shedding the past it has created a historical vacuum upon which totalitarianism can supervene, and in attacking the self or subject it has opened the possibility of an abuse of the

Other because there is *strictu sensu* no Other and no self to be held responsible. Is post-modernism an expression of moral decadence rather than a solution to the problem of decline?[18]

New Age thinking and all that has followed on from it is a direct outcome of post-modernism. The relativism, the lack of historical perspective (or the creation of new myths about the past) and the throwing aside of any sense of responsibility mentioned by Edith Wyschogrod are all too evident. But also clear are its attractions – fun and playfulness, the search for forbidden fruit, the adventure of plumbing the unknown, the acceptance of an eclectic world-view and the lifestyle that goes with it are not to be just dismissed as superficial or self-centred. We shall have to look later at how we can take some of the positive aspects of New Age thinking and seek to speak its language and lead its adherents to the reality of the 'unknown God' who often fascinates them.

Spirituality

Spirituality is a buzz word. Schools suffering an OFSTED inspection are asked about it, celebrities being interviewed are quizzed about it, 'lifestyle coaches' encourage it. Yet its definition is extraordinarily imprecise. Hay and Hunt found that many people outside the Church still muddled it with spiritualism.[19] One of the most succinct definitions, and one which would meet with general acceptance outside the Church, is that given by Gerald Broccoli, 'spirituality is how I make sense of life'.[20] Matthew Fox sees it in wider terms as the interaction of the individual with the universe: 'how microcosm links with macrocosm'. Others see spirituality as having a goal, so Hart and Hartson say more mundanely that it 'moves the individual towards self and community integration'.[21]

The significance of this is seen in the findings of the 2001 census returns in which a specifically religious question was asked:[22]

21 per cent had no doubt of God's existence
23 per cent had doubts, but still believed

14 per cent believed at some times and not others

15 per cent didn't know

10 per cent did not believe in God.[23]

Belief is still around, even if the object of that belief is uncertain. One interesting offshoot of this is the current interest in guardian angels. The idea of heavenly beings, sometimes supposed to be from outer space, is familiar territory for many exploring modern spiritualities. The links with Christian thought are obvious.

Implicit/common/non-religious religion

As a direct result of this spirituality which is 'without form and void' a belief system has developed which avowedly has no connection with any religious institution. This new way of looking at things is called by different titles. None are entirely satisfactory: 'implicit religion' suggests that people have not thought through their personal philosophy; 'common religion' is certainly right in suggesting that this sort of approach is exceedingly common, but suffers from the disparaging other meaning of the word 'common'; 'alternative religion' begs the question 'Alternative to what?'. It does not matter much for all such titles suggest that there is a new religion, with its own doctrines and practice. In fact, individuals make up their own mind, and there are in reality a myriad of 'alternative religions'. While the name may be unimportant the fact that many people now have a self-made belief system which they would hasten *not* to call a religion is vitally important for the Church and its mission.

Many would find it difficult to put their spirituality into words, but this does not mean that it is not real. The issues which people think about and often come to some sort of personally satisfying conclusion about are:

- a sense of purpose in life – our life has meaning, even if we cannot define its nature
- as an addendum to this, life is not snuffed out at death, and there is a common expectation that loved ones (including pets) will be encountered after death

- there is no hard and fast ethical system as far as they are personally concerned (though this does not always extend to their judgement of others)
- institutional religion is rejected as having little to do with spirituality as they understand it
- prayer to someone/something outside themselves is not without meaning.

Lesslie Newbigin even described this substitute for mainstream religions as 'pagan': for him the Enlightenment had led to a new entity which 'is not a secular society. It is a pagan society, and its paganism, having been born out of the rejection of Christianity, is far more resistant than the pre-Christian paganism with which cross-cultural missions have been familiar.'[24] The resistance of post-modern men and women to the desire of the leaders of the traditional mosques/synagogues/churches/gurdwaras to have more worshippers in their buildings as often as possible is unquestioned. Whether this amounts to a rejection of the spiritual is much more doubtful. Even more questionable is whether this may be called, in Newbigin's terminology, 'paganism'. The Hay/Hunt research would suggest that ordinary English[25] people have a lively and enquiring spiritual awareness and that this increased markedly during the 1990s.

Recently there has been published an important postscript which may change our perception. Preliminary findings of a two-year research project by the Centre for Youth Ministry in Cambridge and Theology through the Arts into the beliefs of those born since 1980 (the so-called 'Y' generation) suggest that their awareness of spirituality of any kind at all is very limited indeed. They are interested in 'happiness' with no metaphysical additions. The conclusion of Mike Booker and Mark Ireland is that 'evangelism among Generation Y should not be based on the false assumption that young people have a latent spirituality simply waiting to be activated'.[26] If this is confirmed it adds an important caveat to the Hay/Hunt research.

It is comforting for Christians to think that all this strange spirituality can be attributed to the usual causes of the world, the flesh and the devil. But that may be too simplistic: other factors may be at work.

It is characteristic of post-modernism that men and women are allergic to authority figures, whether they are politicians, scientists, police officers or preachers. They see themselves as autonomous: if they wish to create gods in their own image and worship them, then they are free to do so. But that is not the end of it: they make their own assessment of themselves, whether that is favourable or not. Understanding this is important when we consider a basic religious idea, found in all religions.

The concept of sin

If a religious authority tells a post-modernist, 'You have got it wrong – you are a sinner and have broken the commandments of God', the response is going to be highly negative. If individuals have composed their own spirituality through sometimes bitter personal experience of life and possibly with considerable thought, this appears as an attack on their integrity. To them it sounds as though the authority figure is saying, 'You are a confused fool: I have the truth'. Not surprisingly Big Brother Preacher is rejected with anger and scorn.

In terms of mission this understanding is particularly important where the idea of 'sin' is concerned. When Big Brother Preacher goes on to say, 'You are a sinner, whether you know it or not', it is seen by post-modern individuals as an attack on their sense of self-worth. They may well think of themselves as far from perfect, but they will not accept the title of 'sinner' (and they would not use that word) when it is given to them by someone else: they reserve the right to decide who they are.

This is particularly important because so many presentations of the gospel begin with the reality of personal sin, from which we needed to be saved. Indeed, many of our acts of worship begin with confession: we rightly feel that approaching a holy God requires 'clean hands and a pure heart'. But is this the right approach for people today? That 'there is no distinction, since all have sinned and fall short of the glory of God' is a basic biblical truth (Rom. 3:23). But to realise that presumes both a sense of the presence of a holy God and also the knowledge of our own unholiness.

People accept their personal shortcomings, but to go on to say that they have broken God's laws and therefore are guilty before him is a concept which to many is meaningless. Even for many Christians this Godward element is not present in their repentance. One of the most startling results in my own research was in answer to the question:

> During the period when you professed faith which of the following describes how you felt:
>   (a) I felt a general sense of guilt
>   (b) I felt guilt or shame about something in particular
>   (c) I had no sense of guilt or shame
>   (d) Don't know.

The question was asked because I was trying to find out whether consciousness of sin had been a major part of their conversion experience, for if they had little sense of sin it was likely that the forgiveness offered by God in Christ had probably not been a major factor in their conversion. The results showed that 61 per cent had had no sense of guilt, or did not know whether they had or not (and so it was unlikely to have been deeply significant for them). Of the remainder 18 per cent had felt guilty about a specific matter and 21 per cent had had a sense of general guilt. There was no difference between the sexes in their replies, and the older people were the less likely they were to feel guilty.[27]

I should stress that these were people who had made a recent 'profession of faith' such as adult baptism, confirmation and the like, and many had come from evangelical churches where they would certainly have heard of sin, been taught about its seriousness and invited to repent. Those from liturgical churches would certainly have said some such words as 'I repent of my sins' as they publicly professed their faith. Nor could there be any real doubt of the reality of their faith. My task of reading every one of the 11,000 pages of their responses was like going on a retreat – these were real stories of real people touched by the Holy Spirit. Yet the great majority appeared not to have grasped what is often taken as one of the most basic requirements of becoming a Christian – a 'conviction of sin'. But these people had become Christians and had the courage to say so publicly.

Evangelists may, therefore, have to recognise the fact that a call to repentance from sin may have the opposite effect from the one we long for – that people may turn to Christ. We may even have to face the terrible thought that instead of helping them into the Kingdom we may in fact be barring the door to them.

In future chapters we will try to untangle a Gospel for Modern Men and Women. It must be scriptural; it must emerge from our tradition; it must be effective.

The Adjusting Church

It is too easy to think that the Church has seen nothing, learnt nothing and changed nothing. This is not true: much of this book is seeking to find ways in which the Church can come to terms with both wings, and so fly with greater certainty in the new atmosphere in which it finds itself. There are undoubtedly signs that the Church is beginning to speak in the language of post-modernism:

1. It has become more aware of our emotional and non-intellectual side. The plethora of courses on counselling, inner healing and self-fulfilment show a Church which may even be dangerously over-obsessed with the self, but at least it is change from the situation where all feeling was suspect.

2. It is more prepared to absorb into its bloodstream those move-ments for spiritual renewal which have a more holistic view of humanity and try to combine more successfully the head and the heart. In particular the charismatic movement has been remarkably effective in the changes it has made in liturgy and in engendering a less anxious attitude within worship, not only

among 'card-carrying charismatics' but in churches of all denominations. Further, it has accepted (even, at times, to excess) the concept of emotion as having a rightful place within life and worship.

3. It has begun to accept the feminine more readily. Outwardly,
this is seen in the acceptance of women ministers in nearly all non-
Catholic denominations, but more deeply the equality of women
and men before God has become widely acknowledged, even if
the working out of the principle has by no means been completed.
Sometimes this has led to an excessive compliance with some of
the more foolish diktats of political correctness, but even this
shows that Christians are conscious of the issues involved.

4. There is less concern for theological precision. Some would
argue that this is a horrendous example of the contagious
influence of post-modernism within the Church. Others contend
that if Christians are more concerned to work together to extend
the Kingdom than to wait until they all think alike, this can only
be to the good. It is certainly true in ecumenical work where
the quarrels of the past carry less weight. It is also seen in joint
evangelistic initiatives where churches subsume their theological
differences under a wish to bring the gospel to their community:
often evangelistic campaigns and joint Alpha/Emmaus courses
are far more effective for Christian unity than the usual arms-
length ecumenical conversations.

5. It is noticeable that worship which is clearly not addressed
only to the mind is currently popular. It takes many forms. The
charismatic worship of New Wine and its like is manifestly post-
modern with its repetitive choruses, its mood music, its 'waiting
on the Spirit'. But equally popular is worship which is the direct
opposite to the noise and exuberance of a charismatic service, and
where a profound meditative calm is the main feature. A still more
recent phenomenon has been the sudden popularity of worship
which has a sense of timelessness, such as Orthodox liturgies,
traditional Anglican cathedral services or the occasional Latin
mass held in Roman Catholic churches. At least in part this is
because such worship is *not* immediately understandable and is
redolent of history and an ongoing tradition. Youth services of the

'Rave in the Nave' variety which seek to appeal to the club culture also acknowledge the importance of the non-verbal through their use of current music styles, a strong sense of fellowship with those around them, the mantra-like singing and the use of silence as well as sound. It is sometimes said that these forms of worship are anti-intellectual: it is seldom so – there is nearly always some reading or exposition of Scripture, the prayers are about current concerns, the actual world is not shut out.[28]

6. As part of these new forms of worship, the place of the sacramental is all important. This applies to the greater significance given to the classic sacraments of the Eucharist and baptism, but even more to the rapidly increasing use of sign and symbol in nearly all churches. Sometimes this is the adoption by non-Catholic churches of many practices which were previously thought of as 'catholic': the lighting of votive candles as a symbol of prayer, the use of incense, the greater centrality of the Eucharist, the introduction of palm crosses, the use of the Easter candle. But some symbols are comparatively recent: in many churches the most popular ceremony of the year is the blessing of the oranges at the Christingle service.[29]

While this book argues that the Church should do more to encourage this, we should not be unaware of what is already happening. However, we should not forget that the Church as an institution is still a profoundly modernist organisation in many of its attitudes and methods of working.

CHAPTER 4

An Overview of Evangelism until the 1980s

Why history?

History looks backwards – and it explains the present. It describes what we were – and also why we are as we are. The history of evangelism explains why most of us use certain methods and certain words when we evangelise.

In this chapter we shall briefly examine how a *process* for evangelising came to be evolved, how the *content* of the gospel was honed and how the *response* to the gospel was to be made. We shall primarily examine evangelical evangelism for it was they who took the lead in evangelism, at times being derided and despised for it. However, we should be aware throughout that similar movements took place in other traditions within the Church, especially among Roman Catholics.

In this chapter we shall examine 'classic' evangelism as it evolved in the past couple of centuries until the very recent past. In the next chapter we shall look at the growth of the 'emerging' evangelism which has taken place during the past twenty years in the UK, and now increasingly in the rest of Europe and even in the United States and elsewhere.

It needs to be said by way of apology at the beginning of this historical survey that very little academic research has been done in this field, and much more needs to be done. There may be some excuse for the lack of study of the word 'evangelism', because it does not occur in the New Testament, but the Anglican Report

Good News People[1] points out how little exegetical scholarship had been given to the thoroughly scriptural word 'evangelist', let alone tracing the use of the word through history. It is something of a shock to realise that John Wesley would not have been described as an evangelist by his contemporaries. However, I trust that this outline of evangelism until the 1980s is approximately correct. In many ways we are too close to the 'emerging' evangelism of recent years to see its effectiveness, let alone its long-term consequences, but an attempt must be made to evaluate it, as I have sought to do in the next chapter. This book itself is intended as a contribution to the debate about effective evangelism in the twenty-first century.

Before the eighteenth century

In medieval times the idea of a 'religion' with a corpus of beliefs and practices would have been impossible to conceive. It was the analytical thinking of the Renaissance and greater contact with the non-Christian world which made the distinction possible by the seventeenth century. At the time of the Reformation, if you lived in a certain country you were a Christian – whether you were a Protestant or a Catholic probably depended on its history. For the Reformers, to be a Christian was to be born in a Christian country under the rule of a Christian prince. *The Book of Common Prayer* and the Thirty-Nine Articles of the Church of England are often chided for their lack of missionary emphasis, but in this they were only following the pattern of the reformers on the continent. None of the many Protestant declarations and liturgies of the sixteenth century display any sense of responsibility for mission, apart from a single reference in the voluminous Heidelberg Confession to 'winning one's neighbours'.

Even the idea of responsibility for evangelising the non-Christian world was one which few Protestants were concerned about. In this they were put to shame by the extraordinary missions of the Counter-Reformation Catholic Church which was sending missionaries as far as Japan and China by the 1540s: before long Japanese Christians were prepared to suffer appalling tortures and martyrdom for their faith. It was not until the formation of the Society for Promoting Christian Knowledge (SPCK) in 1699 and the Society for the Propagation of the Gospel (SPG) in 1701 that England began to take some responsibility for mission, and that almost entirely within the burgeoning British Empire. William Carey did not sail to India to begin his momentous work until 1793, more than two hundred and fifty years after the Reformation.

The Christian entrepreneur

It was the energy of Thomas Bray (1656–1730), the Vicar of Sheldon, and a few lay associates which led to the founding of SPCK and SPG.

The Christian Church has always depended much upon the freelance. From its earliest days it has gained immeasurably from the contribution of those with a private fire in their soul.

Paul himself is the archetypal entrepreneur. Once he had the approval of the early disciples he waited for no further ecclesiastical permission.[2] Under what he personally perceived as the guidance of the Spirit he evangelised as he saw fit. He is the prototype of the great Christian pioneers who, on the edge of the Church, have renewed and even revolutionised its life time and again. Inevitably such a process has thrown up the fools and the charlatans and the misguided: the Body of Christ has always had mosquitoes which sting and irritate. But the entrepreneur has always had his or her place, and when this vanguard has been crushed by ecclesiastical authority it has nearly always been to the detriment of the Church as a whole.

Paul worked with a team. As we know from his dispute with Barnabas as to whether John Mark should rejoin their travelling band, it is clear that personal relationships were not always straightforward. Again and again in the early Church we see the idea of the evangelistic group as central to the spread of the gospel. Later it was the monastic movements which carried the flame of Christ to others. Our picture of monks and nuns tends to be of people living in large buildings and keeping themselves apart from the world: we do not see them as trailblazers for Christ. The leaders of the early monks were, however, risk-takers – they hazarded all for God as they disappeared into the deserts and the wild places of Egypt and Syria trusting God for every hunk of bread and sip of water. But then some who had begun by retreating from the world emerged from the silence of the deserts with a blazing evangelistic zeal. Prayer precedes proclamation. Retreat from the world to love God better had become an engagement of love with the people of the world. The anchorites and hermits of the third century had gone into the wilderness places to be alone with God. Their successors of the fourth and later centuries emerged from the deserts to serve and convert the world.

The pioneers par excellence were the early missionaries of the fifth to seventh centuries. I have described in *Recovering the Past* the extraordinary spread of the Celtic monks from Ireland and Scotland into the whole of Europe.[3] From the Ukraine to the tip of southern Italy, from Spain to the plains of northern Europe the Celtic monks ventured for Christ. Usually they went as a small group: the scant literature of the period suggests that three or four was a common number. They set up their hut alongside the villagers and farmed and suffered and rejoiced with them. Being strongly Trinitarian they told the people of the God of gods, of the coming of the Great King of heaven, of the inrushing Holy Spirit. They began to baptise and form a gathering of believers, and once this was established they moved on into a new area: the strawberry plants covered much of Europe.

But the Celts were not the only ones. Augustine and the forty monks with him came to England from monasteries in Italy, Boniface evangelised the Germans with his fellow-monks, founding monasteries to act as centres of influence in many parts of Germany. The monks were the evangelistic spearhead of the Church. Like Paul, once they had obtained the acquiescence of the ecclesiastical authorities, they were on their way. They went into the unevan-gelised areas, to the 'barbarians' of their day – the Anglo-Saxons, the Huns, the Goths, the Vandals. But we should also remember that it was not only the visionaries from outside the ecclesiastical structures who initiated such mission. Popes also wanted to extend the Kingdom. It was Gregory the Great who initiated the mission to England which led to Augustine landing at Thanet in 697. Pope Gregory II sent Boniface as a missionary to the Germans without a specific diocese.[4] Subsequent popes began mission in many parts of northern Europe. The evangelist does not have to be the individual outside the corridors of power: those with a heart for mission may walk the corridors themselves.

Under the hammer blows of the Vikings and the more insidious temptations of power and wealth the early monastic movements lost their evangelistic zeal in the eighth and ninth centuries. But under the impetus of Cluny, monasticism revived in the tenth and eleventh centuries, and from that stemmed many great missionary movements, predominantly the Dominicans and the Franciscans.

In Chapter 7 we shall look more closely at what we can learn from the extraordinary work of the voluntary societies. I shall argue that it is from the different forms of monasticism that we can see some of the different shapes for an emerging and enduring Church for today.

The eighteenth century

If the modern Protestant missionary movement began anywhere it can be located in the Moravian village of Herrnhut in modern Czechoslovakia. Once again the work was pioneered by an individual. The young Count von Zinzendorf had agreed in 1722 to accept onto his considerable estates a small dispossessed band of the 'Unitas Fratrum'.[5] Various religious wanderers joined them and after five years conflict was endemic. As James Hutton, the Moravian historian, writes acidly, 'As the settlers learned to know each other better, they learned to love each other less'.[6] Zinzendorf called for greater unity and the community of about 300 determined to mend their ways and set themselves to pray and seek God. On Wednesday 13 August 1727 at a communion service the Holy Spirit was poured out on them. They called it their 'baptism in the Holy Spirit'. Zinzendorf could only speak of 'a sense of the nearness of Christ' and it seems to have been a time of total surrender to God when, in Zinzendorf's words, 'the Saviour permitted to come upon us a Spirit of whom we had hitherto not had any experience or knowledge . . . the Holy Spirit took complete control of everybody and everything'. Although those present left no detailed accounts of what happened their opponents accused them of speaking in tongues and exercising other charismatic gifts. They covenanted to keep 'the Hourly Intercession' for twenty-four hours a day and 365 days a year: this astonishing prayer meeting went on for a century.

The renewal movement was intensely evangelistic. Soon after August 1727 Count Zinzendorf had, as part of his official duties, to go to the coronation of the new King of Denmark. On the docks in Copenhagen he came across one West Indian slave and two Inuit. All were Christians and they asked for help to be sent to their countries. He told the community at Herrnhut of these encounters and immediately people were sent out to the Caribbean and Greenland. Others followed and within a short while over a hundred people from that small village had gone out as missionaries, many of them to die within a few months of their arrival at their chosen destination.

Of even greater significance was the effect upon other Christian leaders. The case of John Wesley is well known. A Moravian leader in London called Peter Boehler brought the disappointed, dejected John to a full faith in 1738 when his heart was 'strangely warmed'. Less well known is their effect on William Carey, who is often wrongly described as 'the Father of Modern Missions'. Carey himself did not sail for India until 1793, sixty years after the first Moravian missionaries had begun their work. Indeed, in his *Enquiry regarding the Obligations of Christians to use Means for the Conversion of the Heathen* published in 1792 he speaks of the effect that the example of the Moravian missionaries had had on him.

Summing up the work of the Moravians, Kenneth Latourette says:

Here was a new phenomenon in the expansion of Christianity, an entire community, of families as well as of the unmarried, devoted to the propagation of the faith. In its singleness of aim it resembled some of the monastic orders of earlier centuries, but that was made up of celibates. Here was a fellowship of Christians, of laity and clergy, of men and women, marrying and rearing families, with much of the atmosphere. of the monastery and of Pietism, but the appeal of the Christian message as a major objective, not of a minority of the membership but of the group as a whole.[7]

For better or worse (and there are negatives) a small revived group within the Church (an *ecclesiola*) took the initiative without waiting for the rest of the Church (the *ecclesia*). Before the eighteenth century the idea of initiatives being taken without ecclesiastical authority was even more abhorrent to Protestants than it was to Catholics, because at least the latter could channel renewal enthusiasm into a new religious order. Hence, while the tag 'ecclesiola in ecclesia' came to represent a potential for the outward thrust of the gospel, it was far from popular.

Although the word 'evangelism' was used as early as the 1720s to describe a process for helping people to find God through Christ, it was not in widespread use until the middle of the nineteenth century. It was in the young United States that evangelism developed. Despite the religious foundation of many of the states, church attendance was exceedingly low – it has been estimated that at the time of Independence in 1776 only 17 per cent of Americans were members of a church and that the number of people in church on a Sunday was barely 5 per cent of the population. It was little better in England where the doctrinal disputes and wars of the seventeenth century had left a religiously apathetic population and churchgoing was largely sustained by law and the power of the squire. Two names stand out in the English-speaking world as leaders in evangelism in the eighteenth century. In the United States it is Jonathan Edwards; in the United

Kingdom it is John Wesley. In many ways they were similar. Both had a good university education and throughout their lives were concerned that the gospel should have an intellectual content: both of them wrote many books and pamphlets. Both found God through a deep personal experience and both longed that others should come into the same freedom as themselves.

It was Wesley and Edwards who, without realising it, challenged the status quo left over from the Reformation. They could not see any real difference between a nominal Christian and a pagan: as far as they were concerned they were both 'without God and without hope'. They therefore preached that people should come to God and that, if they did not do so, they were not Christians and destined for hell. Hence Wesley's claim 'the world is my parish' did not only refer to parish boundaries in England but made no distinction between home and abroad: both were in need of evangelisation.

The nineteenth century

The birth of modern mass evangelism

Once again we cross the Atlantic. The fires of the First Awakening associated with Jonathan Edwards had burnt themselves out but far on the western frontier there were strange stirrings in the 1790s. The sophisticated Christians on the eastern seaboard heard disdainfully of camp meetings harangued by 'revivalist' preachers accompanied by weird charismatic goings-on and outpourings of religious fervour. Within a few years the camp meeting came East, but it had to be adapted to the social milieu of the population there. The gatherings could not last the two or three weeks which had been common in the West; the meetings had to be shorter; the preaching had to be more polished; there had to be some theological content to the message; and it was important that those who came should not be frightened off by the charismatic.

The person who did most to 'house train' the rough-and-ready camp meetings was Charles Finney (1792–1875). Through speaking, through training young evangelists in his own mould and through his immensely influential books, especially *Lectures on Revivals of Religion*, his teachings had a world-wide effect. Finney did all he could to organise the 'revivals' as the evangelistic meetings came to be called. He was a lawyer, a brilliant administrator and orator and, despite what his detractors said, was by no means deficient in theology. But he thought he could organise the Holy Spirit: one of his books of sermons was called *Sinners Bound to change their own Hearts* (1835): as the title suggests, he put so much emphasis on human endeavour that he was in danger of denying the grace of God and the work of the Holy Spirit. He roundly declared, 'Religion is the work of man', thereby seeming almost to deny any space for the work of God: 'A revival is not a miracle, or dependent upon a miracle, in any sense. It is purely philosophical results of the right use of constituted means as much as any other effect produced by the application of means.' Not surprisingly he strongly discouraged any charismatic happenings which could interrupt the ordered flow of a meeting.

Finney was an activist who presumed that if you did the appropriate thing (the 'constituted means') you would automatically get the desired result from God. He was not a man for *mysterion!* There were three important consequences which still flow from his work:

1. Finney's methodology of the big meeting with the big speaker continues to this day and has spread around the world. Indeed, many people, inside and outside the Church, think it is the only way of evangelising. There have been a long succession of speakers who have used these methods: in our own day some remember such names as Reinhard Bonnke, Billy Graham, Luis Palau and many others.

2. For all evangelists one of the most important issues is how to give people a chance to respond to the message. Finney was one of the first to use the 'altar call'. He wanted the person who had responded to his

preaching to show it by making some physical movement. He recommended that people should move from
their seats and be directed to an 'enquiry room' staffed
by what today would be called 'counsellors'. These
counsellors would ask various questions of the person
who had come forward and, if they responded 'Yes' to
them all and repeated after the counsellor 'the sinner's
prayer', they would be assured that they were now a
Christian. It comes dangerously close to what has been
called 'decisional regeneration' whereby someone is
assured of their rebirth in Christ just because they have
repeated a certain formula. Although the use of the altar
call became almost normative for such evangelists, by
no means all were persuaded. Charles Spurgeon
(1834–92) asked people to sit where they were and
pray, 'Lord, save me tonight'. In one of his sermons he
pictured someone saying 'I should like to go into the
enquiry-room'. Spurgeon responded robustly, 'I dare say
you would, but we are not willing to pander to popular
superstition. We fear that in those rooms men are
warmed into a fictitious confidence. Very few of the
supposed converts of enquiry-rooms turn out well. Cast
yourself on Christ ere you stir an inch!'[8] It is interesting to
reflect that the altar call was unknown to Edwards,
Whitfield or Wesley – let alone St Paul.

3. Finney was a systematiser. He wanted to devise a clear-
cut pattern which could be used again and again with
different people to bring them to Christ. In particular, he
wanted to have a series of questions which he could
train counsellors to use in the enquiry room so they
could help people to faith. Wesley had had only the
simplest of patterns of 'faith development' – conviction
of sin; new birth; sanctification: joining a Methodist
church usually came before the experience of new
birth.[9] Charles Finney developed a much more detailed
list of experiences which the prospective convert had to

go through. It began with a 'concern' about one's state before God, which led in turn to 'inquiry' as to the truths of the gospel. Knowing these, one was led into a state of 'anxiety' as to one's eternal destination in heaven or hell. The process climaxed in 'conviction' where the penitent, realising that only full and complete (and instant) surrender to Christ would avail, 'received Christ' at the 'anxious bench' at the front of the meeting. Conversion had to be clear and dateable so that the new convert could look back and realise that it was on such and such a day that he or she became a Christian.

There is a direct line of descent from this simple pattern to the 'Four Spiritual Laws' and the ABCD of the gospel which I can remember being taught as a new Christian: Admit you are a sinner; Believe in the gospel; Count the cost of discipleship; make a Decision.

This pattern, pioneered by Finney, became, with few alterations, the mainstay of 'mass evangelism'. There is no doubt that it is a process which has genuinely brought many millions of people to God over the past two centuries. But there are negatives:

(a) The personality of the preacher can get in front of the person of Jesus Christ. Too often it has seemed as though the preacher is saying, 'Look at me'. The antics of such evangelists as Billy Sunday (1862–1935) brought little glory to God: his 'blazing-fisted, bare-handed evangelism' is a part of the history of Christian America, but even America tired of him after the First World War.

(b) There is the constant danger of manipulation. The power of 'brain-washing' was first seen in its effects on prisoners of war in the Korean war, and the setting of the big stadium can be conducive to contrived reactions. In my experience the reality of manipulation is a good deal less than is often thought, but it always has to be guarded against. Nevertheless, the procedures of the 'enquiry-room', which it is hoped that everyone who responds will go through, can be dangerously lacking in integrity: no one person responds to the love of God in Christ in the same way as another and to treat all alike is to show a lack of respect. It is true that 'all have sinned and fall short of the glory of God', but it is illegitimate to argue from this scripture that each individual's route to the forgiveness of the cross should be the same as everyone else.

(c) The danger of exaggeration is ever present, particularly in the published statistics of those who have been converted. All research suggests that only a fraction of the proportion of people who are claimed to profess conversion actually show it by a marked difference of lifestyle.[10]

(d) While it is true that the financial cost of such campaigns is high, possibly even more demanding is the amount of Christian time and energy which has to be put into counselling, stewarding, administering, etc. For churches putting their weight behind a campaign it may well mean that they are unable to undertake any other initiative for a year or more.

(e) Evangelism of this kind is directed to the conversion of the individual. Since the preaching of the Kingdom with all that means in terms of corporate responsibility and regeneration is largely omitted in case it clouds the clarity of the gospel, the accusation is often made of a lack of social concern, but in my view there is not always much substance to it. While it is true that it may not have been at the forefront of the evangelist's preaching ministry, it does not mean that there were not social challenges as a result of such evangelism. In the 1830s Charles Finney insisted that his colleges for preachers should be open to blacks as well as whites. No one could accuse William or Catherine Booth of forgetting the social context of their ministry, for from the time of their first revival meetings in East London in 1865 the need for accompanying social action was stressed by them both. Despite his questionable presentation of evangelism as a vaudeville act, Billy Sunday insisted on non-segregated congregations when he preached in the South and campaigned vigorously for votes for women. Billy Graham has done much to challenge the prejudices of the southern states in which he grew up. Indeed, because of the accept-ance by so many ordinary Christians of the words of these evangelists it is possible that they have done more to challenge and change such prejudices than more intellectual approaches.

The need for mission

Mission leaps to the head of the agenda when it is seen that the Church is failing; at other times we too easily enjoy ourselves with our own affairs. The broadcaster Gerald Priestland said of the Church of England, 'It is a very laid back church: it gets its thrills from frightening itself to death!' All denominations towards the end of the nineteenth century were beginning to scare themselves about the decline in churchgoing, which began in the 1850s where the Church of England was concerned, and in the 1880s for the Free Churches. It began to be recognised in the UK that the 'work-ing man' had largely forsaken the Church, especially in the new industrial cities: there were even debates as to whether or not he had ever been there.

This led, in the Evangelical, Tractarian and Modernist move-ments, to a desire to bring the gospel to the bulk of the population. A welter of voluntary societies were founded which tried to touch one or two particular elements in the population – child chimney-sweeps, deep sea fishermen, prostitutes (many societies for these!), Cornish tin miners and so on: it was a Victorian example of niche marketing. Some of them still remain: such organisations as the Church Army have flourished, while others have either dwindled to nothing or merely to the publication of a poorly produced magazine.[11] But these initiatives were not left just to the entrepreneurs: the denominational structures themselves were alarmed. Some thought that the problem was a lack of church buildings and so churches sprang up throughout the new cities: the Bishop of Lichfield launched a passionate appeal for money for he wanted the whole population of his diocese to be able to sit down on an Anglican pew at the same time. The relics of this boom in church and chapel building (often in bickering competition) are still around us. It was not just buildings for people, especially clergy and ministers, flooded into the previously neglected places and a ministry in some such place as the East End of London became almost a required part of a clerical CV.

The twentieth century until 1985

By the middle of the twentieth century 'crusades' were an accepted part of the Christian scene, although largely ignored by the church establishment: the involvement of Michael Ramsay, then Archbishop of Canterbury, in the Billy Graham campaigns[12] showed some change in attitude in the UK, but generally most in the Church saw them as crude and simplistic and best left to evangelicals.

It was clear that the move away from the Church which had so exercised the Victorians, was continuing inexorably. While it has been shown that the commonly held assumption that men lost their faith in the trenches of the First World War is a myth,[13] there is no doubt that churchgoing steadily declined. The rate of decline varied, and there seems to have been an acceleration of the decline after 1980 despite the Decade of Evangelism.

By the 1980s the loss of members, the resulting financial pressures and the obvious lack of penetration of the population at large meant that most denominations were taking evangelism seriously and there were an increasing number of experiments and fresh thinking.

There was also an increasing questioning of 'words only' evangelism. The importance of the Church as a vehicle of the gospel began to be taken seriously and it was no longer seen as just an unfortunate appendage of the good news. This did not prevent an increasing torrent of words. In 1900 the gospel was proclaimed only by public speaking and the printed word, which had been around for 400 years. Technology began to produce a flood of fresh possibilities. The less highly regulated American scene was able to take advantage of the new media as soon as they became available. In the 1920s came radio. Almost as soon as public broadcasting began it was used for Christian ministry: the first broadcast came from Episcopal Calvary Church in 1921, and by 1927 there were more than sixty Christian stations in the US. The use of film as an evangelistic medium began when Billy Graham showed excerpts of his latest crusades in 1950:[14] he also used widely the 'share-a-thon' which asked listeners to send money to the station for the support of its work. This financial influx meant that, when much more expensive television became available a few years later, it could be exploited and the 'electronic church' was born. This has been defined as 'all electronic communication that is generally perceived by senders and receivers alike as religious in intent and content'.[15] Though its detractors thought that this inevitably meant that fewer people went to a 'real' church, research showed that it seemed to have little effect at all.[16]

The rise and fall of the televangelists in the US has been often told. By 1980 Jerry Falwell had the widest syndication of any television programme, religious or secular. He and the networks run by such people as Jimmy Swaggart, Oral Roberts, Jim Baker and Pat Robinson had blanket coverage to proclaim not only a religious message but also a political one, and they became one of the most influential of the political interest groups, particularly during the presidency of Ronald Reagan. They also made a serious amount of money. In the late 1980s came a series of scandals which undercut their influence and closed many of their networks.

Beyond the TV station came the use by Christians of video as a vehicle for evangelism, the distribution of the *Jesus* video in 592 languages being one of the most significant. Hard on its heels has come the Internet, which after faltering early steps became increasingly important with the publication in 1996 of Mark Keliner's book *God on the Internet* who described it as 'one of the greatest mission fields in history'.[17] Christians have increasingly made use of the new medium, and there are now Alpha and Emmaus groups which have been formed on the Internet. One Emmaus group links together in one chat room people from New Zealand, England, Texas and Canada. In May 2004 came the launch of virtual church services organised by the Internet organisation Ship of Fools, at which the Bishop of London preached the first sermon.

The position of evangelicalism

Evangelicalism deserves a note of its own, for of all the strands in the Christian rainbow it is the one which has adopted modernism most wholeheartedly, especially in its American form. Andrew Walker comments too accurately for comfort: 'Modern evangelicals have unwittingly adapted to the privatised, individualist and subjectivist strands of structural pluralism and recast Christianity not as an inculturated grand narrative for the modern world, nor even as a domesticated sitcom for the local churches, but as therapy for the lost and sick, the unhappy and the repressed.'[18]

Too easily evangelicals adopted modernist management techniques, seen most clearly in the Church Growth thinking which embraced Management by Objectives just as MBO was fading from fashion among the management gurus. It has sought unrealistic verbal precision in its doctrinal statements just as contemporaries were deconstructing the very language which was being used. In its attempt to make worship 'meaningful' it has too often adopted a style which is redolent of the chat show or the singalong, forgetting that media styles are essentially ephemeral.

It is not surprising that many American evangelicals have had the greatest difficulty in coming to terms with post-modernism and have been unable to take it seriously. Even today the outlook of many of them is shaped by a view propagated by many excitable TV sermons and especially by the genre of Christian novels that sees the Rapture as imminent and New Age spirituality as being of the devil.[19] This has been compounded by the tendency to stamp with the same satanic 666 such matters as ecology and global warming, nuclear disarmament and peace rallies, alternative lifestyles and medicine, and even meditation and contemplative prayer. Hence the religious right in America has too often attacked evangelicals who have tried to discern what New Age thinking means and how a post-modern culture can be approached evangelistically.

CHAPTER 5

The New Evangelism

Evangelism in the last twenty years

In 1985 evangelism for most people still meant the big meeting, the imported speaker, the exhausting (and expensive) effort by the church. By 2000 evangelism in the United Kingdom meant the small group, the ordinary member of the congregation, the continuous work of the church.

It was sensational. It had happened without anyone really noticing it. A few evangelical leaders like Gavin Reid had been saying that reliance upon the big campaign was no longer appropriate. The Decade of Evangelism had meant that non-evangelicals who had tended to turn from evangelism with a shudder were now examining it more closely. But there was another reason why it changed.

Basically, it did not work. As we have seen in Chapter 3, the spiritual context of the United Kingdom has changed radically.

Evaluation of evangelism

For all those wedded to the *kerugma* approach to evangelism, people needed to hear the Word of God, and then repent and believe. It was quite simple. This being so, then evangelism was getting as many people as possible to hear a preacher. The more famous the preacher the better since more people would come to hear him (it nearly always was a 'him') – and so began the process which was codified by Charles Finney. It needed a lot of organisation and required a certain technique. Since there were not many preachers known outside the Church (basically Billy Graham), we had to get him to come. Because he could only come for a short time we had to provide the largest venue that could be found and filled. Hence, Harringay and Wembley and the football stadia were filled by Billy Graham from the 1950s to the 1980s.

After the big Billy Graham campaigns in the 1980s they were evaluated. People sat down and worked out how effective they had been, not just in giving the local churches a shot in the arm (which was undeniable) but by asking how many new people had really come into the churches as a result of the enormous expenditure of effort and money. The results were inevitably mixed. Quite a number on the edge of the church had found a deeper commitment to God and were more regular in their attendance. But although there were some complete outsiders who had found Christ and become disciples the numbers were not great. Looking back on the campaigns of 1984, 1985 and 1989 Gavin Reid, the chairman of the British organisation which invited Billy Graham, says: 'I felt we had been involved in a very successful mission. I was equally sure, however, that we had not tapped into the soul of the nation in the way that Graham's 1954 crusade had done. The world was now a different place.'[1]

But the Billy Graham campaigns had introduced a comparative novelty to the British churches – what was called the 'nurture group'. It had been used in Graham's mission in Australia, but was greatly developed in the British missions of the 1980s. In reality, as we shall see, such groups were not new to the British Church. Further, they were not originally intended to lead to conversions. The intention of the Billy Graham organisation was that those who had 'gone forward' in the stadium should be channelled into a group so that they could be more securely anchored in their local church. Hence, the teaching given in the groups contained such themes as assurance of faith, reading your Bible, Christian fellowship, and so on. They were not intended to lead people to Christ – but they did.

Moreover, churchgoers who were involved in the groups discovered a new boldness. They found they could sit in a room with a group of fringe churchgoers and even with non-churchgoers and talk about the faith and see some become Christians. It was not necessary to invite someone from outside to come and do their evangelism for them.

Ironically, while the Graham campaigns of the 1980s showed us the ineffectiveness of mass evangelism in reaching non-Christians in today's climate, they also revealed the way ahead to us. It was a pointer of the Spirit.

Before examining the nurture courses it is worth pausing to consider the need to analyse evangelism because this change from the stadium to the nurture group gathered pace as a result of just such an evaluation. Too often Christians fail to analyse. Three criticisms are often levelled at those who make this sort of judgement. Let us say that an analysis of Method X shows that in most situations it is ineffective:

(i) Analysts, because their role is to examine a particular method of evangelism, are too easily seen as being against any form of evangelism – and so seem to join the ranks of those who criticise the very idea. They can be accused of turning traitor just because they suggest that the evidence is not there to continue with the effort and expense of Method X.

(ii) Those who are committed to Method X may accuse the analyst of being unspiritual by failing to recognise the spiritual battle which is being waged. Method X is considered to be failing to bring results because of 'the hardness of men's hearts' rather than there being a recognition that it may not be appropriate for that time in that place.

(iii) It is sometimes supposed that if you don't think about something it shows you have more faith. If you question the conduct of worship, it shows that you are not really worshipping. If you think about how the Christian faith is expressed, you are monkeying with the creeds and are clearly a dangerous liberal subversive. Evaluating evangelism is doing the devil's work.

Faith does not equal foolishness; thinking about evangelism is not dangerous: it is essential. If we do not evaluate, we shall not just waste money and time: we shall also lead many Christians to become disappointed and disillusioned, for flogging dead donkeys is a discouraging business.

The nurture group

The history of the nurture group

The rise and rise of the nurture group is a phenomenon which has had a massive impact on the Church in the UK and, increasingly, on the Church worldwide. In a period during which bandwagon after bandwagon (mainly American) has influenced church life in the UK – power evangelism, cell church, Toronto, Willowcreek, etc. – the humble nurture group, which began in the UK, has itself become a prominent bandwagon. It is now a worldwide phenomenon and it can certainly be argued that it has been more evangelistically effective than many more high profile movements.

It can be traced back to the catechism and confirmation groups and the membership classes which had been a normal part of church life for generations. But it was the recognition of the differences in the evangelistic context of the UK which led to the start of the nurture group. There were four factors:

(1) For generations many good catechisms and confirmation courses had been produced for the training of young people. However by the 1960s it was realised that there was an increasing number of *adults* coming to faith who had probably not been baptised as babies, nor attended any Sunday School, nor been confirmed as teenagers. How were they to be introduced to the faith and helped to make it their own?

(2) The 1960s saw the rise of 'inchoate spirituality'. It was the age of flower power and the aimless spiritual search, usually seen in terms of self-fulfilment. Confirmation classes and the like were designed for those

who had already made up their minds. Now churches encountered an increasing number of adults who wanted to explore the 'spiritual', but were certainly not prepared to make a commitment to faith before they found out more about the Christianity they were being invited to believe in. An almost new group of people had emerged, who came to be called 'enquirers'.

(3) The 1960s and 1970s saw the burgeoning of the charismatic movement in the mainline churches, and those involved felt that the existing confirmation courses on the market did not cater for this new insight into Christian initiation. Many churches influenced in this way wanted a course which would introduce existing church members to the work of the Holy Spirit. Influential in this was the 'Life in the Spirit' seminars which were produced in America in the late 1960s to introduce members of existing Roman Catholic prayer groups to the charismatic dimension. It began to be used by other denominations. However, this course and others like it were not evangelistic – it was assumed that the members of the group were Christians. Moreover, a theological change was taking place. The Pentecostal churches taught a two-stage initiation – conversion followed by 'baptism in the Spirit' – but many mainline charismatics disagreed and thought they saw in Scripture that Christian initiation was a single event. Thus, they considered it wrong to teach a group about baptism in the Spirit without also teaching about conversion: conversely, they did not want to bring new-comers to faith in God without also telling them about the baptism in the Spirit. Therefore, the groups run by charismatic churches were essentially evangelistic.

(4) Ordinary pastors had long realised from their ministry to ordinary people that the initiation of an individual into the fullness of God was a good deal more complex than just 'going forward at a meeting' and something

deeper and more extensive was required. As William Abraham says:

> Initiation involves a complex web of reality that is at once corporate, cognitive, moral, experiential, operational, and disciplinary. Initiation into the Kingdom of God is not only one of these; nor is it all of these strung together as a mere human enterprise driven simply by earthly passion and planning; it is all of these set and bounded within the dramatic action of God that is manifest in Christ and fueled by the Holy Spirit.[2]

Ministers struggled to adapt the traditional confirmation courses to the new reality, but they usually failed to make the transition from teaching a lively group of eleven-year-olds to dealing with the questions of an adult group. Moreover, they found that a different teaching style had to be used with adults – they had to be less didactic and the experience of group members had to be incorporated. Churches began to produce programmes to cope with their own needs. Courses with titles such as 'Agnostics Anonymous' or 'Just Looking' were produced by local churches to fill a local need. Particularly significant was the course produced by St Margaret's, Nottingham which was run repeatedly with different parish groups during the 1970s. In 1983 an adaptation of it was published as *Saints Alive!* by Anglican Renewal Ministries. Despite its low budget production it was used by more than 250,000 people.[3] At much the same time *Good News down your Street* by Michael Wooderson was published and widely used. Both courses were developments of initiatives which had been tried and tested in ordinary Anglican parishes. Both of them looked for those who attended not only to come to faith but also to experience the power of the Spirit.

As we have seen, a further step forward was taken during the Billy Graham campaigns of the 1980s. It was felt that many British people were so far away from the faith that, after making a decision in the stadium, they needed to be steered towards a small group for learning and integration into the church. They proved their worth: research after the campaigns showed that 72 per cent of people who went to a nurture group went on to full membership of their local church while only 23 per cent of those who did not join made that transition.

It was through these campaigns that the 'nurture course' got its name. The Billy Graham course for follow-up assumed that the people who came to it had already made their 'decision for Christ' in the stadium: it was intended to strengthen those who had recently come to faith. For this reason it was called a 'nurture course': i.e. for the teaching of those who had already been born again and needed to grow. However, the term 'nurture group' stuck, despite the obvious fact that 'nurture' refers to the period *after* birth. These evangelistic groups could be more accurately described as 'maternity wards' since they are to do with new birth in Christ as well as growth afterwards.

In 1991 the Decade of Evangelism was started with varying enthusiasm by different churches. Those who had been given responsibility for steering the Decade met regularly under the chairmanship of the great Methodist statesman Donald English. Despite considerable pressure we determined that the main emphasis for evangelism in England should be the nurture group rather than the big national evangelistic campaign. This led to such headlines in the Christian press as 'The Decade begins by not evangelizing!'[4] Local churches were encouraged to set up their own nurture groups to draw in those outside the church.

My own research into what actually happened to people who became Christians showed that it was a more complicated process than had been supposed and also that it often took place over a period of time, sometimes many years.[5] It was published in 1992, and during the same period the Anglican House of Bishops set up an enquiry into the whole subject of Christian initiation and its influential report *On the Way* was published in 1995. The title is indicative of the new thinking. Conversion was no longer seen as a sudden decision by an individual who stepped from unfaith to faith in a moment but as a pilgrimage where each individual came to faith by a different journey.

The *Alpha* course thus fell into fertile soil. It was started by Holy Trinity, Brompton in London in 1977, but initially was intended only for those who had already become Christians: in other words it was a 'nurture course' in reality as well as name. Later, in the years after he came to HTB in 1986 to work with John Collins and Sandy Millar, Nicky Gumbel changed the nature of the course, making it more directly evangelistic. It was published for use beyond HTB in 1993 and since then its growth has been phenomenal. Translated into many languages it has been used by millions of people throughout the world. Although now published by Alpha International it still has close links with HTB, and, quite rightly, the use of the course with ordinary people in that church still influences its development.

Others were working along the same lines. In the 1970s the Roman Catholic Church had produced 'Rites for the Christian Initiation of Adults' which envisaged a considerable period of time when a newcomer could learn and experience the faith, and RCIA became part of the normal life of many Catholic parishes. The ecumenical Catechumenate Network drew together those who looked for inspiration to the training methods used by the Church in the third and fourth centuries: this early catechumenate required that those coming to faith from paganism be prepared for two or three years before baptism.[6] The stress which the early Church put on proper Christian initiation and the effort and prayer which was required is seen as a guide for the twenty-first-century Church when once again people are coming to faith who have no Christian background whatsoever. It also reminded churches which had thought of evangelism as merely a peripheral activity how central to the life of the Church the making of new Christians should be.

These different streams of experience and thinking resonated in the Wakefield Diocese. Churchgoing in that area was among the lowest in the country, and many people were at least 'four generations' from faith. Thus:

Generation 1: Parents and children attend church. All have some knowledge of the faith.

Generation 2: The children, now grown up, do not go to church themselves, but send their children to church. All have some knowledge of the faith.

Generation 3: Those children, when they grow up, do not send their children to church. Only the parents have some knowledge of the faith.

Generation 4: The next generation have no contact with church whatsoever, apart from an occasional funeral or wedding. None have any knowledge of the faith.

The result was the ebbing away of any knowledge of the basics of the faith: the biblical stories were not known and words like 'cross' or 'Easter' had little or no emotional resonance for people. The reason for the church building being there was not known. It forms a pattern of decline in awareness of Christianity.

Those of us in Wakefield realised that for people who are 'Generation 4' or beyond a fifteen-session nurture course was not sufficient. There had to be a continuing process of Christian discipleship which might even need to match the timescale of the early catechumenate. Because of this the Wakefield diocese produced the *Emmaus* course: initially intended for local use, it is now published worldwide. It has a 'nurture' section, very similar in content and length to *Alpha*, but continues with some fifteen other short courses (in all some sixty-four sessions) which both help the newcomer to get a rounded view of the Christian faith and also keep them within the supportive fellowship of a group.[7]

There has been a variety of other courses, most of which have their roots in Christian adult education and/or the charismatic movement, though a few, like the fourteen-session *Christianity Explored*, come from a more conservative evangelical background.[8] Of particular interest is the *Essence* course which seeks to form a group from those who have had experience of New Age practice and method.[9] Most courses have an evangelical background, though *Credo* is Anglo-Catholic in origin, and *Emmaus* prides itself on having its genesis in several traditions. *Emmaus, Alpha* and others have also produced versions suitable for young people.

The result is that churches have the choice of a number of different courses. Indeed it has been found that, since the nurture course is intended to be used repeatedly with different groups, the leaders become bored with one course and need to change to a different one for the sake of their own sanity!

Evaluation of nurture courses

A number of research projects have looked at the significance and impact of these courses. Their findings have been excellently summarised by Charles Freebury in *Alpha or Emmaus?*[10] which, while concentrating on the two named courses, also refers to the others which are available.

At the end of 2003 Christian Research published the booklet *Leadership, Vision and Growing Churches*,[11] which is an account of research carried out for the Salvation Army looking into the life of 1125 churches, one of the largest samples yet attempted. The main findings of all this research can be summarised:

(1) Approximately one in six of those attending the courses say that they have become Christians as a result. Since over 2 million people have attended these courses over the past ten years, it means that in excess of a third of a million adults have become Christians through them.

(2) There now appears to be considerable difference in the evangelistic effectiveness of the different courses. The Salvation Army research gives the percentage of 'faith commitments' as being:

	Alpha	Emmaus	Y Course	Good News	Christianity Explored
Churchgoers	17%	38%	18%	24%	22%
Non-churchgoers	45%	50%	38%	50%	27%

It is encouraging to note that virtually all the non-church-goers were still attending church six months later. Of parti-cular interest is the fact that a considerable number of churchgoers had come to faith through attendance at a course: the assumption is too often made that those who are coming to church do not need an opportunity for commitment.[12]

(3) Thus, while the courses were written primarily with non-Christians in mind, they often have a profound effect upon existing church members who attend them, and through them the worship, the outreach and the morale of the church are affected for good. Thus, while the courses are largely designed for individuals, the cor-porate impact can be considerable.

(4) When a course is repeated there is a change in the dynamics. Often the first course is composed almost entirely of church members, and the more committed church members at that. It usually goes well: excite-ment is high, and many are helped and enter into a new phase of their Christian life. However, when the course is repeated for a second and third time there can be a considerable fall both in the numbers attending and in the level of enthusiasm. There is, therefore, a strong temptation for a church to say, 'This does not work for us' and to stop running courses after the second or third repeat: some estimates put the number of churches which do this as high as 50 per cent. Nevertheless, it has been found that it is when a course has been run four or more times that the numbers of newcomers increase and the course begins to impact the whole life of the church. Numerical growth is stimu-lated or decline slowed.

(5) Most courses assume that they will be run by a single church. In reality many courses, especially *Alpha* and *Emmaus*, are run by several churches ecumenically. As Charles Freebury says, 'Every church that had held

their course inter-church reported that the course was better for it.'

(6) The number of churches using these courses seems to have levelled off since 1998, and churches seem to be looking for something which is less dominated by the agenda of the church and more by the wishes of those taking part. Two factors seem to be leading this quest. The first is to do with method: is a group of people sitting round a Bible the way in which people learn these days? The *Essence* course seeks to combat this by providing touchy-feely 'New Age' ways of learning through sight, sound, smell and touch. Secondly, there is a questioning of whether it is right to put the need for repentance from sin as up-front as many of these courses do. In an age where the idea of guilt before God is a strange or even bizarre concept for many, should some other aspect of the character of God be emphasised? Is showing God as Saviour the right launch pad for the gospel in an age which is more interested in God as Creator or as Guide or Protector?[13] This is explored in detail when we look at the 'Athenian Gospel' in Chapter 6.

(7) The need for adequate follow-up after the course has ended is shown by all surveys. It is pastorally criminal to help someone to find faith within a warmly supportive group and then disband it at the end of the course, with nothing to put in its place.

(8) Only a third of churches in the UK use a nurture course, which means that the rest are missing out on one of the most effective means of evangelism.

This leads us to a question which is seldom asked: why are nurture groups apparently thriving these days? We have seen the advantages and disadvantages of mass evangelism: why have these groups become so effective – and what are their limitations?

Why are nurture groups successful?

The positive

(a) *They are built upon relationships.* The way in which the members interact with each other is crucial: when asked at the end of a course, 'What part did you enjoy most?', by far the most common answer is 'being together'. Many then go on to praise the openness, the laughter and the social life of the group. The *Alpha* course recommends that each time a group meets they should have a meal together, and certainly the friendliness of the group should be seen as of almost equal importance as its spiritual life – indeed, it is difficult to separate the two, for Christianity is a corporate religion. In these groups people do not only make friends with God, they also make friends with each other, and their spiritual growth occurs alongside the social interaction. In particular, the relationship with the leader is all important. Adults learn from those they trust and respect: the smoothly insincere salesperson puts our backs up. In the New Testament the most prominent requirement of Christian leaders is that they should be 'faithful': the root meaning coming from the Greek word for 'believe'. Thus leaders are asked to be 'trustworthy', 'believable', with all that speaks of dependability, care and thoughtfulness.[14] The *Finding Faith Today* research showed that about 80 per cent of people point to a relationship with another person as the main reason that they became a Christian.

(b) *They are relaxed but have a goal.* Educational research shows that adults learn best when (i) they are enjoying themselves, and (ii) they have a goal to achieve. Purposeful fun is a potent mix: think of the amount of energy and concentration which is given by a group of people who set themselves a task – whether it is building a machine to take part in the television programme *Robot Wars*, organising a local horticultural show, or taking part as a team in a pub quiz. Incidentally it is interesting to see the reaction in those situations to group members who just want to theorise or argue – they are resented because they are seen as holding up the completion of the task: the same is true in a nurture group – someone who just argues for argument's sake is not regarded as a helpful member of the group.

An important by-product of this educational task is the view of God and the church that is gained. Many non-churchgoers associate God with gloom – they only come into contact with God at funerals and on tourist visits to shadowy churches. Being in a brightly lit and comfortable room resounding with peals of laughter teaches them that God is a God of happiness and life. Similarly churchgoers are often portrayed on the media as dull fools or cranks, and coming into contact with Christians who are manifestly normal and interested in ordinary things can exorcise many of these negative mental images.

(c) *They are group-based but church-linked*. A nurture group should not be separate from the church: it should be owned by the church, encouraged by it, and seen as an important element within it. Many of the people who come on such courses come because they made contact with the institutional Church through attending a service, wanting a baby baptised or attending a funeral.[15] At the same time it should not be controlled by the church, so that it is not free to experiment: some of the best groups are made up of people who do not fit easily into the life of a traditional church – they may be young people with ideas of their own, or those coming to faith from a New Age direction or those who have no idea of church traditions. The job of the group is not to make people conform to the social and theological norms of the church but to help the church to accept and learn from what the new people can teach them – and possibly change as a result.

(d) *They do not dictate how people find God*. All the research shows that people come to faith by a myriad of ways, for the 'narrow gate' has many paths leading to it. A nurture group should not be manipulative and expect people to go through a certain pattern of behaviour when they become Christians. For example, it has been found that 31 per cent of people have a sudden conversion and can give the date on which they became a Christian. For the other 69 per cent it is a much more gradual process, often taking years. A nurture group should not demand that members follow any particular spiritual pathway, but allow them to explore and discover the Christ at their own pace.

(e) *They blend reason and experience.* In Chapter 3 we looked at the bizarre bird which represents present-day ways of thinking with its two ill-matched wings of modernism and post-modernism. People want to have reasons for believing, but they also want to experience something for themselves. A nurture group will be together for many hours and should come to the point where members trust each other enough to be able to talk about some of their own adventures along the spiritual road. At the same time testimony by itself is not enough – there has to be teaching and the opportunity to chew on subjects until they become clear. Educationalists distinguish between 'separate' knowing which is modernist in its approach – impersonal, analytical, uninvolved – and 'connected' knowledge which is post-modernist in its emphasis on experience and the uncritical acceptance of ideas. The educationalists go on to suggest that neither is enough in itself and that a synthesis of the two produces 'constructive' knowledge, which melds theory and experience.[16] Needless to say, this is something that the nurture group leader should also strive for because it links mind and spirit together into a unity in Christ.

(f) *It gives space for the work of the Holy Spirit through other people than the leader.* One of the most difficult parts of group leadership is to be able to delegate control to another. Particularly if leaders are nervous, there is a tendency to want to make sure that nothing goes wrong. In a group this often results in leaders who:

(i) talk too much – for if others are given room to talk they may not follow the pathway the leader wants to go down.

(ii) ask a question and then answer it themselves: members are not given time to formulate their own answer, for silence is seen as extremely threatening.

(iii) fail to see the work of God in other members of the group. Often this happens because leaders are so concerned about their own performance that they are not aware of what is happening within the others.

(iv) fail to give space for prayer and an invitation to the Holy Spirit: 'Come, thou Holy Spirit, come' should be the prayer of every leader. Leaders should also pray that they may have the discernment to see the ministry of the Spirit when it happens through other people.

(g) *They are often lay-led*. When nurture groups start in a church, a frequent pattern is that the first course or two is led by the minister, hopefully with lay help. But later they are run almost entirely by lay people. One of the most important by-products of such courses is that there is a growing body of lay people who have seen God at work, who have helped others to come to God in Christ, and have had the spiritual responsibility for a group of people. The long-term effects of this cannot but be beneficial.

Every group leader has a story of their group. May I humbly contribute mine:

We met in a room which led off the bar in a pub. There were about ten of us gathered around a table. At half-time we had a break, and the group went into the bar and most came back with pints in their hands: but that was not all, for when they went through to the bar they met some of their friends and invited them to come and see what was happening. As a result, after the break, besides the ten round the table there were seven others leaning against the walls. Our discussion continued where we had left off, and at first only group members spoke. However, after a few minutes first one and then several of the newcomers joined in. Their comments were not critical, but genuinely wanting to find out more. We went on long after our planned closing time, until the landlady came and shooed us out.

A few months later I met the wife of one of the newcomers who said that her husband had become a Christian as a result of that night: she commented, 'He only asks questions when he has a couple of pints inside him'!

The negative

I am passionate about nurture courses: I have had a hand in writing two of the most widely circulated courses, and I have spoken and written enthusiastically about them. But we must not put all our eggs into this basket. We also learn when we look at the negatives.

(a) *Groups are artificial.* Although a great deal of church practice and adult educational theory is based upon the idea of a group of people gathered together, we should not forget that a group brought together for teaching or discussion is basically a contrived construct. Whether we are thinking about an adult education class gathered to learn French or a church group meeting to learn about the Christian faith, it is not the way most people encounter each other most of the time. Usually we gather in clumps – small groups outside the school gate, chatting over a cup of tea, exchanging stories in the pub or round the coffee machine in the office. It is in these natural gatherings that we need to be able to gossip the gospel. The group meeting is not a natural way in which we interrelate, however useful it may be for educational purposes. Few of us from church or educational backgrounds cannot but echo with a sigh the wise words of an expert: 'Discussion groups can very often be an effective way of increasing individuals' contributions, but it can look like a stale, manipulative device, an application of group-dynamics for the sake of applying the theory rather than because it answers the students' needs.'[17]

(b) *Groups only attract the curious.* A vast number of people in this country go to work in the morning, come home, watch the television, do DIY and never go out except for family excursions to the shops or on outings or to see other members of the family. They belong to no organisation, join no group, seldom go to the pub: they are self-sufficient. They do not want to learn anything else nor do they want to meet new people. They would not dream of joining a group, especially not a church group. The only means of contact the church might have with them is through those in their workplace or through other members of their family.

(c) *Groups only attract the gregarious.* A lot of people are loners, self-conscious, awkward in strange company, frightened of joining a group of any kind. Not all churchgoers are particularly group conscious: even when a church has a well-established house-group structure research shows that seldom do more than 25 per cent of the congregation belong to any group.[18] The church has to be aware of the non-joiners and those who like to keep themselves to themselves.

(d) *Groups suit the educated and articulate.* Others can feel out of their depth.

(e) *Nurture groups may be post-modernist in their approach but their content is usually modernist.* The agenda is set by the 'leaders'; a book is often used; there is a pattern which is generally adhered to. Truly post-modernist courses begin with the agenda of the participants, are usually not constrained by a book and can wander where the group wants.

The Church has always hoped that it would find one answer that would evangelise all people. Enthusiast though I am, I have to admit that the nurture group is not the answer for everyone.

It is important that, when we go on to think about the emergence of new forms of evangelism and what the content of that evangelism should be, we think carefully about these five negatives, for they apply to all too many of the means of mission which we employ.

Nevertheless, there is no doubt that the advent in many churches of the nurture group has made a very considerable difference to church life in the UK and, increasingly, in other parts of the world. It has given the privilege and responsibility of evangelism back to ordinary church members. It is right to end with a comment on the effect of leading such a group: Brian McLaren writes in the delightfully entitled book *More Ready than you Realise: Evangelism as Dance in the Postmodern Matrix:*

If we engage in spiritual friendship with others, if we try to help others become disciples, we find our own under-standing of what it means to be a Christian changing. We will see our lives as a dance to God's beautiful song, and we will feel it our incomparable honour through spiritual friend-ship to help others feel the song's wonder and be swept up into its graceful beauty and resounding joy.[19]

CHAPTER 6

Evangelising Athens – Then and Now

Chapter 2 looked at the essential unity of evangelism, whether it is seen in terms of *kerugma, evangelion* or *mysterion*. In Chapter 3 we investigated the context in which the gospel is to be proclaimed in the twenty-first century. In Chapter 4 we saw how the good news of Jesus was made into an easily memorised and preached evangelistic message which had been packaged in a thousand different wrappings but with the same inner content. In Chapter 5 we traced the recent rise of the nurture group and other forms of evangelism which are less prescriptive about what the gospel is, and which move in the area of *mysterion* as well as *kerugma* and *evangelion*. Now we think about the *content* of the message of the gospel which we take to those outside the Church.

Later chapters will examine how the ideas set out here can be worked out in practice. Can we change our evangelism to be more 'intelligent and effective'?[1] But our thinking cannot stop there for these ideas have implications for the shape of the church and its leadership. Making this sort of mission a priority means that the whole life of the church has to be adjusted to take account of it.

'Finding Faith Today'

When we researched how adults come to faith, the results were published in two forms. The first was the 'popular' version of the research which was published under the title 'Finding Faith Today'. But that was based on a much larger document called *The*

Technical Report which was written by Pam Hanley, the excellent professional researcher we had employed. This Report was only of interest to statisticians and those academically interested and was never widely available. I gutted it and made it the basis of *Finding Faith Today*.

Inevitably much of the material in the larger Report had to be missed out. Rereading the Report later I realised that one interesting response had not been included in the shorter book, and that it had a deeper significance than I first realised. Those being questioned about the time when they had 'turned to God' were asked: 'Did you find any parts of the Christian message particularly appealing?' There were no boxes to tick – each person was left free to make their own contribution.

They answered:

God's love	mentioned by 14% of the respondents
Particular Bible passages	13%
Forgiveness	13%
Death of Christ	8%
Life after death	8%
Helping other people	7%
God always there	6%
Jesus' life and example	5%
The resurrection	2%
'Nothing in particular'	16%

As I reread these results I was struck by how few mentioned the cross of Christ and the forgiveness of sins – only 21 per cent. Yet many of those answering the question came from evangelical churches and other places where this would be expected to be the normal understanding of Christian discipleship. Apparently four-fifths of people coming to faith did not find the cross and forgiveness the most appealing part of faith.

When this is put alongside the fact that we also found that 61 per cent of people said that they felt no sense of guilt when they came to faith, we can see that the appeal of the Christian gospel is by no means confined to the message of sin and salvation *even to those who do become Christians.*

Little other research has been done in this area, but there is anecdotal evidence which suggests that the forgiveness of sins is not the main attraction of the gospel for all those who come to faith. This is particularly true of younger people whose whole life has been spent in a post-modern world of relativism and uncertainty concerning truth. As one 24-year-old man said to me, 'Sin and repentance just do not grab me – if I talked about it at the office they would think I was nuts.' Yet I could not doubt the reality of his faith, for the light of Christ shone in his eyes as he was baptised: for him it was the towering love of God which had embraced his soul.

A defence

Before going further I need to make a statement. I am conscious unless I do some readers will not be able to hear what I have written in the rest of the chapter.

I believe entirely in the atonement made on the cross for the sin of the world. I believe that the cross is central to the gospel, and I believe in the need for repentance and the acceptance of the forgiveness of God. I believe in the assurance which God gives to those who repent and believe.

All I am saying in this chapter is that the cross has an even wider significance than the forgiveness of sin, and repentance is more than saying 'sorry'.

I believe that in our proclamation of the gospel we have too often made our wondrous God 'too small'. The Creator of the universe is more than just a Saviour, glorious though that fact is.

We get scriptural support for this from the startling story of Paul's visit to Athens.

The Athenian gospel

Is this the story of one of the worst evangelistic sermons ever preached?

A so-called preacher is addressing a large and influential New Age congregation. He does not begin with any biblical text, but dwells on a particular New Age symbol. He not only quotes various New Age gurus, but agrees with them. He does not quote the Bible, he does not use the name of Jesus, and he gives no account of the cross and the atonement. He adopts a sort of universalistic stance and assumes that all his hearers are on their way to God: indeed, he praises them for their religious zeal. At the end of this feeble effort he asks them to respond. Rather surprisingly some do.

This is, of course, a jaundiced view of Paul's evangelistic address in Athens in Acts 17.

In Acts, Luke gives us an extended outline of only two of Paul's evangelistic sermons.[2] The first is in the synagogue at Antioch (Acts 13:16–41) and gives us an example of his style before a Jewish audience. It is stuffed with biblical references; it gives an account of the life of Jesus and the reaction of people to him. It is a logical piece of exegesis. It ends with a proclamation of the forgiveness to be attained through faith in Jesus.

The second example of an evangelistic address is that before a non-Jewish audience in Athens. It is startlingly different. The fact that Luke includes it at such length suggests that Theophilus and we are intended to learn from it. As Walter Klaiber says,

> The prominent location and the fact that this is the only sermon Paul preached to the Gentiles which Luke reports leads to the supposition that he attributes programmatic meaning to this speech. Thus Paul preached in the stronghold of education in Greece, and thus one should preach before educated Greeks.[3]

The visit of Paul to Athens recounted in Acts 17:16–32 is the only reasonably full account of Paul speaking to a non-Jewish audience.[4] Before this, in Salamis and then in Antioch, in Iconium, in Thessalonica and in Beroea we have seen him speaking to the Jews. Usually he had preached in the synagogue. Sometimes there had been non-Jews who had also heard and sometimes become believers, but the main thrust of his teaching was to the Jews. When he came to Athens he had begun in his usual way, 'So he argued in the synagogue with the Jews . . .', but then he moves outside the religious space into the open air, '. . . and in the market-place every day with those who happened to be there' (v. 17).

It often happens that, when you take one opportunity to witness, another presents itself. Paul was given an opening which he took with both hands. In the market-place where he was speaking were some 'Epicurean and Stoic philosophers'. They politely asked him to come before the Court of the Areopagus so that he could explain himself. Part of the duties of that Court was to check on what was being said within Athens so that nothing seditious or dangerous to 'religion' could be promulgated. Those who brought Paul before the Areopagus were taking a considerable personal risk. If Paul, with his talk of resurrection, had proved to be the deranged buffoon ('this babbler'[5]) that some had suggested, they themselves would have been made to look thoroughly foolish: he must have impressed them.

What Paul says before the Areopagus is remarkable. When he first came to Athens he had been sickened by the number of idols in the place (v. 16). The Greek word used to describe his feeling is *paroxusmos* – the word has been translated 'irritated' which is feeble in the extreme. The translation in the New Revised Standard Version is 'deeply distressed' which is nearer the mark. The word means that the sight of the idols sickened him to the core of his nature: a paroxysm is not a momentary reaction.[6] Walter Hanson described it as a 'spiritual revulsion against the ubiquitous idolatry in Athens'.[7]

Paul, as a good Jew, would have argued that at the heart of idolatry is the desire of human beings to manipulate God. Isaiah had long ago pointed out with caustic humour that idols have to be made and therefore are ultimately under human control: 'he makes a god and worships it' (Isa. 44:9ff.).

For Paul an idol was a flagrant breach of the second commandment. It would have revolted his Jewish soul. Yet he had seen them
before often enough – after all he had spent months in Antioch
where they were commonplace. We do not know exactly why he
was so appalled by them in Athens. It may have been that their
sheer number showed him the spiritual void in the intellectual
centre of the world; it may be that the myriad of prayers being
made to them revealed a frantic people who sought but never
found.

As author, Luke puts in an ironic comment at this point: 'Now
all the Athenians and the foreigners living there would spend their
time in nothing but telling or hearing something new' (v. 21). We
know that, among the philosophies which proliferated in Athens,
one would gain a temporary popularity only to lose it to the allure
of the next new idea. Athens was the home of dilettantes, and they
were as ready to embrace novelties as some thinkers are today.

And, extraordinarily, it is with that unclean thing, an idol that he
begins his address. As Martyn Atkins says:

> Paul, a Jew, a Pharisee, a walking law machine . . . who
> knows that monotheism and a rejection of idolatry are the
> bulwarks of faith . . . walks into an unclean Gentile environ-
> ment, sees a graven image to an unknown God and
> comments to his hearers how much they share in
> common! Make no mistake, today's equivalent is a
> Methodist minister walking into a witch's coven and
> declaiming, 'I see we share an interest in spiritual things'.[8]

Good preachers have always known that they should begin where
their audience are at. This is doing it with a vengeance. He
comments that they are 'extremely religious' – because they have
so many idols! Preachers who wish to relate to their congregation
often tell of some incident 'while I was on my way to church this
morning'. Paul goes one better – he uses the episode where he saw
the 'altar with the inscription "To an unknown God"' as the mainstay of what he says.

As we have seen in Chapter 2, the revealing of the *mysterion* to individuals is the hidden work of evangelism. God reveals himself. In the Old Testament we see this through the uncanny wandering lights which Abraham witnessed in Genesis 15, through the stranger wrestling with Jacob at Peniel in Genesis 32 and through the bush 'which was blazing, yet it was not consumed' which Moses encountered in Exodus 3. These are 'theophanies' – times when God becomes apparent to human beings.[9] The New Testament is about a permanent theophany – the incarnation of Christ. But even after his advent there are particular theophanies to individuals: on the road to Emmaus, Clopas and his companion met the Stranger who only revealed himself when it was right to do so: before that moment of revelation 'their eyes were kept from recognizing him'.[10] In a theophany it is always God who takes the initiative in disclosing himself.

It is the One who is this unknown God (*agnostos theos*) that Paul introduces to the members of the Areopagus. Interestingly he gives no name to *agnostos theos* – the name of Jesus is not mentioned throughout the sermon: he is only alluded to as 'a man whom he [God] has appointed'.

Paul goes out of his way to carry his audience with him. He begins by declaring that gods do not need shrines 'made by human hands' since God is far greater than any local deity. God gives to all people everywhere their very subsistence and 'allotted the times of their existence and the boundaries of where they would live'. He quotes from two Greek poets and states that 'we ought not to think that the deity is like . . . an image formed by the art and imagination of mortals'. Up to now most of the Areopagus would have been nodding their head. Few educated Greeks believed in the reality of the Greek pantheon with its disputatious gods and their all-too-human love lives. However, they knew that the social cohesion of Athens was strengthened by a common belief, and so the worship of the temples was encouraged: it was for this reason that they were both suspicious of and yet interested in Paul's teaching: it was more than a casual inquisitiveness.

Paul first excuses them and then challenges them. His hearers were not guilty because they had not realised before what the truth was, for 'God has overlooked the times of human ignorance'. But that time was past: now the time for repentance had come, for the world is to be judged by this unnamed person whom God has appointed. Furthermore, God has shown his endorsement of this person and 'given assurance to all by raising him from the dead'. The resurrection proved that he really was from God.

There are several startling omissions in this discourse. There is the lack of any personal testimony. In other settings Paul made full use of his own experience. Before the hostile crowd in Jerusalem in Acts 21:37–22:16 his vision of Christ on the Damascus road was the focus of what he said. Before Agrippa he gave his whole curriculum vitae starting with his upbringing in Jerusalem right up to his current ministry to the Gentiles (Acts 26:1–23). But he knew that before the sophisticated Greeks he needed more than his personal witness to Christ. He desperately wanted the gospel to be taken seriously by these influential people and he was trying to convince them that he was as rational and well educated as they were, and stories of a light 'brighter than the sun' and voices from heaven would not have been helpful.

But that is less significant than the theological omissions of the Athenian discourse. There is no mention of the incarnation, of the atonement, of the need for salvation, of the coming of the Holy Spirit.

He concentrated on the idea of theophany. He was speaking to an audience who were used to the idea that God revealed himself, for the Greek gods were always showing themselves to mortals, sometimes in human form and at other times as creatures like swans or eagles. Probably few of the Areopagus would have taken these tales seriously but they were used to the idea of revelation – gods were expected to disclose themselves.

It was the idea of this theophany through the raising of a man from the dead which divided them. In the market-place a little while before, it was the proclamation of the resurrection which challenged and divided. It was the same at the Areopagus. They certainly did not throw Paul out – some thought he was talking nonsense while others were sufficiently convinced to want to find out more.

Paul adapted his message to his hearers. He took into account their education, their social background, their standing in the Athenian community, their interest in philosophy and rhetoric, their ambiguous relation to the official religion of the day. Earlier when he had gone to the Jewish synagogue in Athens his message would have been much the same as the one he had preached in the synagogue in Antioch. Now, in front of the Areopagus, he proclaimed a very different message.

It is sometimes said by those who think the Areopagus address is theologically suspect that it was so unsuccessful that he never preached a similar one again. This is hard to sustain. Luke goes out of his way to say that 'some of them joined him and became believers, including Dionysius the Areopagite and a woman named Damaris and others with them'. To have converted one of his judges and someone who was clearly a woman of significant social standing could hardly be called non-productive. Indeed, it is hard to see why Luke would have included it at such length if he thought it had brought no results.

To summarise: Luke gives two of Paul's public evangelistic discourses in Acts:

1. *The address at Antioch in Acts 13:13–41.* It is at the very beginning of the first missionary journey. It is given in a synagogue, and is packed with references to the Old Testament and to his hearers' place within the covenant. It speaks of sin and the salvation brought through Jesus Christ. Here Luke seems to set out the normal Pauline gospel which he preached to the Jews, a sermon Luke must have heard many times.

2. *The Areopagus address in Acts 17.* It is not in a 'church' setting and is given in front of a non-Jewish audience. It is vastly different in tone, in content and in style to the sermon in Antioch. There are no references to the Scriptures, no mention of the place of the Jews in God's

plan of salvation, not even one mention of the name of Jesus Christ. Luke seems to be showing how adaptable Paul was to a different context, and in particular to the Gentile world.

Antioch and Athens

Modern evangelists all know that they must change the method of approach according to their audience: a group of youngsters demands a different style and technique than a group of academics. But usually the message which the evangelist is trying to get over is the same in either case – it is to do with sin and salvation. The language used may be different, but the content of the message is much the same each time.

The New Testament seems to suggest otherwise. It is impossible to extract from the words of Jesus in the Gospels any formula of salvation. He speaks *ad hominem* – adjusting his words to the needs of his hearers.

In the same way Paul's specimen sermons at Antioch and Athens show not just a difference of style but a greatly different *content*. Yet both addresses are evangelistic because on both occasions Paul is preaching for a decision. Indeed, it is one of the few common factors to both sermons. At Antioch he says: 'Beware, therefore, that what the prophets said does not happen to you', and in Athens he says, 'God . . . commands all people everywhere to repent.'

The question many modern Christians need to face is, 'Have we assumed that the good news which is rightly given to Antioch is also appropriate for Athens?' Have we taken it for granted that a gospel whose content was suitable for the church is also satisfactory when the message is taken out of the church?

Our 'church' gospel has focused on the great truths of incarnation and atonement, of human sin and salvation. Indeed, as we saw in Chapter 4, in some evangelical circles it has almost been reduced to a formula. Church people and those who were brought up in the life of the church are familiar with the words preachers use and the worldview from which they speak. There is even a comforting familiarity in such words as 'cross', 'repent', 'the blood of Christ' and in a Pentecostal setting they will elicit many a loud 'Amen' and 'Alleluia'.

But that seems to cut little ice with those not brought up in Christian surroundings, where the words we use and the way we say them are strange indeed. Sin is barely thought about, and certainly is not seen in biblical terms as a falling short of the glory of God. Salvation, whether through the cross or in any other way, is not a concept that worries the modern mind. Credal statements are seen as semi-mythological – rather similar to the way in which the monarchy is regarded – impressive but unreal, having the trappings but without the power.

Have Christians, because it makes us feel safe, adopted a 'one size fits all . . .' approach? Have we made our gospel too small by restricting it to a few wonderful elements within the Scriptures but thereby failing to convey all the fullness of the biblical message? 'They can have any colour provided it is black' may have been all right when the Ford company began, but they soon discovered that in the long run it did not sell cars.

Paul had the courage to take an almost completely different approach when talking to Gentiles. He began where they were, entered into their thought patterns, built upon their existing beliefs, treated them with respect. If the idols which revolted his soul were important to his hearers, then he was prepared to meet them halfway, talking about them unemotionally and respectfully but pointing out their deficiencies.

Nor, of course, should we assume that Paul had just one 'Athens' sermon. Probably the message he preached to the Jews in Antioch had many of the same themes as those he preached in most synagogues when he went to a new town: after all they shared with him a common religious background and a common knowledge of the Scriptures. But the message he preached to the Gentiles would have to have varied greatly according to the people he was addressing. Athens in front of the Areopagus was one thing; Athens in the market-place would have been quite different – the rough and tumble and bustle of the ordinary citizens of Athens was far different from the thoughtful calm of the Areopagus. The judicious comments of the Areopagus would have been worlds apart from the obscenities launched at him in the market-place.

We can visualise, therefore, a single more or less unchanging 'synagogue' gospel for 'Antioch' and a wide variety of 'Gentile' gospels for Athens and the like.

Conclusions

What can we piece together from this look at the Pauline preaching? Tentatively we can suggest the following:

1. When we are evangelising those involved in the life of the church, who know the basic message of the Bible and understand the language of sin and salvation, then we should have a 'Gospel for Antioch', which builds upon that knowledge and challenges the hearers to repentance and faith.

2. When we are evangelising the '4-generations +' people who do not have this basic knowledge and biblical background, then we must copy Paul and adapt our message as well as our methods to our hearers.

3. Before he spoke to the Greeks Paul listened to them: he had known their language since boyhood but he had also studied their literature and understood their religious longings and philosophies.[11]

4. Like Paul we should build upon the belief patterns of an audience. Educated Athenians had a half-hearted faith in idols, a love for the Greek poets and a belief in deities who revealed themselves in human forms. Paul entered into their way of thinking as far as was consonant with truth. Only at the end of his discourse did he introduce the controversial idea of the resurrection. Christians may need to relearn this. Some evangelism is confrontational – the image is of one person challenging another face to face. Paul's did not set out to be deliberately disputatious.

Mentally he walked side by side with the members of the Areopagus as long as possible.

5. Christians must not avoid the encounter with different opinions. The views of those we meet may be far different from our own. Paul grasped the opportunity of appearing before the Greek rulers and his address certainly gives the impression of having been prepared well beforehand: with its apposite quotations from the poets and the careful build-up of the argument it does not seem to have been extempore. At times Christians give the impression of wanting to duck encounters with atheists or members of another faith or those with a philosophy of their own. Paul had sufficient confidence in the gospel to be prepared to argue the case for it.

6. Paul treated the ideas of others with respect. Even to those who practised the idolatry he loathed he spoke sensibly and logically. He had learnt from the Hebrew prophets to rubbish idols with scornful laughter, yet he treated idolaters with respect and we can learn from the way he handled himself. Despite his personal deep distaste for idolatry, he spoke about it straightforwardly and calmly. Christians today in the smorgasbord of beliefs find many opinions they disagree with wholeheartedly and even come across views they see as dangerous or even satanic. They meet the weird and wonderful in the New Age; they come across members of another faith who think Christianity is inferior to their own. We may have an emotional aversion, just as Paul did to the idols of Athens. For the sake of those in need of the gospel we should overcome our emotions. We need to hear the great affirmation of Paul on the subject of evangelism:

> I have made myself a slave to all, so that I might win more of them. To the Jews I became as a Jew, in order to win Jews . . . To those outside the law [i.e. the Gentiles] I became as one outside the law . . . so that I might win those outside the law. To the weak I became weak, so that I might win the weak. I have become all things to all people, that I might by

all means save some. I do it all for the sake of the gospel, so that I may share in its blessings.[12]

It is the cry which comes from the heart of any truly servant evangelist.

Putting it into practice

To proclaim a wider gospel which can be heard and responded to by modern men and women requires a considerable change of approach from preachers and evangelists.

It does not, of course, mean that the themes of sin and salvation are no longer appropriate: there are still Antioch situations which demand a clear and challenging portrayal of God as Saviour.

However, an Athens address to an audience which is in part non-Christian may well start from a different aspect of God's multifaceted being. A few possibilities are worked out in detail in Appendix A:

1. The God of Creation — let us worship with thanks-giving
2. The God of Hospitality — let us enjoy his company
3. The God of Mystery   — let us explore that mystery.

There are also suggestions of many other elements of the being of God which might be used as the basis of our evangelism.

CHAPTER 7

A New Monasticism

'*Start with the Church and the mission will probably get lost. Start with the mission and it is likely that the Church will be found.*'[1] This quotation from *Mission-shaped Church* puts succinctly the right way to approach the issue of how the Church of the future will emerge from the present. Make mission the priority and let the shape evolve as is appropriate.

We have found in previous chapters that the church is all too often disregarded because it is seen as being (a) irrelevant to people's everyday lives, and, more painfully still, (b) irrelevant to people's spiritual needs.

What shape should the church adopt for the twenty-first century? Structure is important: our skeleton determines the sort of shape we are. But our bones do not determine our smile or our frown: those come from our personality. Just getting the structure of the church right is not enough – the 'personality' of the church is also important. There is the danger that we create an organisation which is as smooth running and impressive as a Formula 1 car – but which is just as impractical for ordinary people's needs. Indeed, the New Testament suggests that 'personality' is much more important than shape for it tells us very little indeed about the structure of the early Church: the Gospels provide us with no clue at all as to how the Church was to evolve as an organisation. Even Acts and the epistles give us only a sketchy view of what was happening in the newly founded churches. It may well be that different 'shapes' were evolving in response to the different environments and cultures around the Mediterranean, and so the hunt for a single New Testament pattern of church government is a hopeless pursuit for a will-o'-the-wisp.

As we look at the whole of the New Testament we find little interest in the structure of the church but much concern about the 'personality' which was to evolve within the church – 'This is how you should behave towards each other'; 'This is how you will grow mature in Christ'; 'This is the effect of the work of the Holy Spirit among you'.

The structure

Before we look more deeply into possible structures we are faced with a difficult question: 'How far should the church mirror the society around it?' There are two ways to look at the question:

(1) Should we look at it horizontally, from the point of view of the consumers – both those who are already within the church and those we hope will come to be part of it?

(2) Or should we look at it vertically, from God's point of view?

There are many possible horizontal models, mainly leading from Church Growth principles and the models of those who propound the 'Seven Principles which are guaranteed to make your Church Grow' schools of thinking. One of the best analyses is that given by Steven Croft in *Transforming Communities*[2] who has helpfully set out different views of the church *from the point of view of the consumer.* Thus we have:

- *the church as a chain of cinemas* – people go if they like the programme, but have no loyalty to any particular cinema chain

- *the church as a local franchise* – consumers go to sample what a 'successful' church elsewhere has found to work

- *the church as factory* – which tries to produce more disciples of Christ. Part of this way of thinking is 'quality control' which seeks to ensure that the factory is efficient and positive, and often auditing their structures by using such patterns as 'Natural Church Development'

- *the church as a mirror* – which replicates the surrounding culture so those who go feel at home.

There are a number of other possible patterns of church life which have been suggested, many of them stemming from the work of Peter Rudge in his seminal book *Ministry and Management*.[3] In 1968 Rudge set out five basic models of church life and the different theologies which lay behind them. However, we also need to hear his warning that 'sociological inquiry has shown that, irrespective of source or doctrine, many churches have assumed a common organisational character'. It has to be admitted that despite the different philosophies which lie behind many modern churches they all look remarkably the same – the Common Denominators at the moment seem to be:

(a) a certain style of entrepreneurial leadership which means that the church is led by someone who can be described as a 'Shaper', who can envision and enthuse, think laterally and be able 'to explain where the church is going, and to do so in a few crisp words'[4]

(b) worship which is imaginative and lively, and which will vary from service to service and from week to week

(c) a cell structure which may be either an effective house-group structure or the adoption of a more self-conscious Cell Church pattern. This will be allied to regular nurture groups of the Emmaus/Alpha kind

(d) a vigorous pattern of teaching and involvement for children and young people

(e) a building which speaks of modernity, welcome and comfort

(f) a spirituality which is easily absorbed and easily practised.

It has to be said that this image of the church may be more popular among ministers than among lay people. Furthermore, it is not as radical as is sometimes supposed – in fact, it is just a more up-to-date expression of a form of church life which has been around for generations. All six of the above could easily have been the aim of a forward-thinking minister in the 1960s or 1970s.

While there are obvious strengths in terms of relevance and energy in the consumer-led models, there are uncertainties about their spiritual richness. As John Drane says,

> A McDonaldized existence is less than fully human . . . Though pre-packaged consumerist spiritualities (both Christian and others) may appear to work for a time, they will not ultimately quench the spiritual thirst of the human spirit any more than the non-stop consumption of food or household goods can meet the fundamental needs of those who are struggling to make sense of the personal emptiness that can be induced by a commercialized commodity culture.[5]

If a church is seen purely from the point of view of management and customers, the vertical Godward dimension can be forgotten. Numerical growth can seem to be the deciding factor. It seems from what we have seen before that the world outside the Church has already discerned this truth about the Church: it is not spiritual enough. The world looks for spirituality and the Church does not satisfy that need. As Michael Ramsey said, 'We have been dosing our people with religion, when what they want is not that, but a relationship with the living Lord'.

However, there is another pattern of church which starts, not from contemporary culture or from the belief that 'the customer is always right', but from the being of God. In other words it begins with the vertical rather than the horizontal.

The nature of the church based on God is less clear-cut than the consumer model. It finds itself circling around certain foci:

1. At the heart of the Trinity are interrelationship and fellowship, for each element in the divinity is both separate and

yet united. The careful distinctions made by the early Church Fathers as they teased out the credal statements about God come into their own here, especially their thinking about the *perichoresis* – the interaction between the persons of the Trinity. A Christian is not only an individual but also part of a corporate whole. The church must, therefore, be based on community and life within that community. The essential corporateness of the New Testament understanding of church points in the same direction.

2. At the same time God is essentially One. The church which is modelled on his being will seek unity. This does not just mean the worthy but apparently unending gyrations of ecumenical 'high-level' conversations but the seeking by individual Christians to overcome fissures and confusions between themselves and others who bear the name of Christ. Above all, as the New Testament epistles repeatedly stress, it is the seeking of unity within the local church.

3. God is a missionary. We would not know God unless he had sent his Son and the Holy Spirit. The Trinity is not a closed circle but blazes with an outflowing love. The Church modelled on the *missio dei* will be giving itself away in service to others. Hence, there will be the twofold longing – on the one hand to share with the world for whom Christ died the good news which has meant so much to them, and also a desire to serve the creation without thought of return. Further, since God's love streams from the vulnerability and openness of the cross, the church itself must be open to and experience the pain of the world.

4. The Holy Spirit pulses with the heartbeat of the Godhead, so a church reflecting the being of God will be one which is both open to the Holy Spirit and prepared to listen to the voice of God. It will therefore be a naturally 'spiritual' church in which the relation between human beings and

their Maker is seen as central. Consequently, it is bound to seek to be obedient to the will of God.

5. Christ obeyed the Father: 'I have not spoken on my own, but the Father who sent me has himself given me a commandment about what to say and what to speak.'[6] An obedient church, it will be filled with a God-given faith, and will therefore be prepared to take the risks inherent in faith.

6. The equality of the persons within the Godhead will be reflected within the structure of the church. There should, therefore, be no striving for pre-eminence, no favouring of one person or class of people over others and no hierarchy of authority. It will be the antithesis of the managerial style which the world too often suggests as the best method for the government of an organisation: as Jesus warned his disciples: 'it is not so among you'.[7]

It has often been remarked that the structure of the church has nearly always reflected the prevailing social pattern of its day. In Roman times the position of bishops mirrored that of contemporary government officials; in the Middle Ages the pattern was feudal while since the Reformation democratic ideas have become paramount. Nor do we just have to look backwards to history. More than a few traces of Communist authoritarianism are still retained by churches in Russia and Eastern Europe, while African church leaders have some of the characteristics of tribal chiefs, and American churches reflect the competitive diversity of their society.

This may not necessarily be something to be deplored. If a church is to fit into its surrounding society so that it can minister effectively, then it may well need to accommodate itself to that society. But there is an important corollary: if that society is changing fast, then the church itself should expect to change fast.

But is the church to be horizontal or vertical in its structure? Most models offered to us today are managerial, while the 'Godhead' model is less precise and less easily copied: however, it can be argued that it is certainly more attractive theologically and more likely to show to others the reality of 'being church'.

To start with it is important to avoid unhelpful polarisation. There can hardly be a horizontal church which does not have some vertical component, or a Godward church which totally avoids some aspects of management and awareness of the 'customer'. However, there is a real difference: some churches so emphasise the human aspect that God is brought in as an afterthought; there are also churches which so emphasise the Godward that they do not engage with the reality of the world around.

Certainly it will be easier for the Godward church to engage with the issues that seemed so important to St Paul. At the heart of his thinking was the 'personality' of the church, and a glance at the second half of nearly all his epistles shows that for him the heart of the church was community and how Christians behave one to another. As Gilbert Bilezikian says, 'the making of community cannot be a side issue or an optional matter for Christians. It is as important to God as one's personal salvation. Without community there is no Christianity'.[8]

For Paul the churches to which he wrote were to be 'colonies of heaven'.[9] What shape are these colonies to be?

The rebirth of the monastic community

Sixteen hundred years ago Augustine and his monks came from Rome to evangelise South-east England. At much the same time a swarm of Celtic monks came to evangelise the rest of the Anglo-Saxon kingdoms. As I pointed out in my book *Recovering the Past*, it was the Celts with their flexible ways of working, their preparedness to take risks (sometimes none too sensible) and their eagerness for God who did most of the evangelising. The Roman communities founded upon Benedictine principles were always in two minds: on the one hand, there was the desire to go out and evangelise, but there was also a countervailing attitude which asked that the monks should stay within the mother house: in the end it was the latter which triumphed and was enshrined in the laws of the Synod of Hertford (672).[10] It may be that we need to learn from the Celtic rather than the Roman attitudes.

The heart of a monastic community, of course, is a group of people with a common commitment to each other and to the task of the community. While we often think of the members of such communities as living under one roof, this is not necessary as the multiplicity of 'Third Orders' testifies. These usually undertake a common Rule of Life, and sometimes meet occasionally, but are otherwise physically separated. Indeed, some of them have members scattered around the globe. What they all have is a common aim and a common fellowship. Together they are the flowering of a new monasticism.

The Third Orders suggest a further important point which is likely to become more important with time. Many people are members of more than one community. It is possible to be a member of the Franciscan Third Order and also a member of the local church community. It is also already the case that many Christians look to their engagement with New Wine, Soul Survivor, a retreat centre or Walsingham as an important part of their spiritual life which goes alongside their membership of a local church. When we look at the possible models of community it is important to realise that they are not mutually exclusive – indeed, several of them almost demand that those who belong to one community also are part of another.

I would suggest there are five possible models of community, and all of them I would be prepared to dignify with the name 'church'. For too long we have seen the local church and its support structure, whether Presbyterian, independent or Episcopal, as the only real church. I would suggest that the emerging church will be less restrictive and more prepared to accept other patterns of church: at the end of the chapter I will spell out the significance of this change. Some of these paradigms look very like extensions of present patterns of ministry, while others may be less familiar.

1. The *spiritual* community

Many existing religious communities are made up of people who have drawn aside from the world in order to be with God. From the Carthusian monks to the Celtic hermits men and women have felt this call of God. These communities know about God, about the spiritual walk, about the battles against evil and the sinfulness of the human heart.

In a world which is desperate for spiritual depth these communities and others which might be formed have much to teach. Unfortunately, they too often minister only to Christians who go to them to draw from their spiritual wells, and they nearly always do so within a church context. In an emerging church whose heart is missionary this may no longer be sufficient. I would like to see community members in their distinctive habits talking to young people in schools and colleges, conducting retreats for non-Christians in places with no ecclesiastical overtones, being a Christian presence at Body, Mind and Spirit gatherings. Many they would help and some they would bring from unfaith to maturity in Christ: is there any greater task for any Christian?

Moreover, they would return from their engagement with the spirituality of today with ideas and ways of thinking which could be of the greatest help to the whole Church.

Community members would need to be firm in their faith but flexible in their thinking. It would require communities which were generous in sharing their members with the world and prepared to allow experimentation and bold thinking. Above all they would need to resist the temptation to retreat into their 'safety zone' by ministering only to Christians and within the environs of the church: the caution of the Synod of Hertford must not again be allowed to stifle evangelism.[11]

2. The *incarnational* community

This pattern of church life is probably the most familiar. The incarnational community is part of a geographical area and seeks to serve the wider community within that area. Just as Christ came to a certain people at a certain time so there is the need to minister to a locality. Even Christ seems to have set boundaries at times – 'I was sent only to the lost sheep of the house of Israel'[12] – and there are times when boundaries can strengthen. The disadvantages are well known: as Robert Warren says, 'the genius of the parish system is that it was a brilliant expression of how to be Church in a non-mobile, hierarchical, feudal society'.[13] It has to be said that, despite these drawbacks, the system is remarkably resilient and is still the 'default mode' for nearly all denominations. This suggests that it may have more spiritual strength than simply being a residue of the past, however frayed at the edges it may sometimes appear. It is sometimes criticised for inflexibility, but we have to recognise that one reason for its persistence is its elasticity. It can adapt to its surroundings so smoothly that a suburban church in South London can look vastly different from one ten miles further north in the Docklands or ten miles further south in a Surrey commuter village.

We shall have the incarnational church with us for a long time to come. Other forms of being church may supplant it in the end, but the idea of a fellowship of people serving those around them in the name of Christ is not an ignoble one. Further, since it is the pattern of much of the present Church, I do not think that we gain much by rubbishing it as no more than a historical relic before we have a firmer view of what will take its place as a basis for evangelising the country and building up the people of Christ.

There are certain dangers which have to be fought against. The first is obvious: a parish has boundaries but, as has been said, 'the minister's job is not to defend his parish but to serve it'. Boundaries can be overcome, but an effort has to be made to do so. The second danger is that of petty hierarchies where the local church becomes a place for power struggles and jealousies: it has ever been so, as we can see from 1 and 2 Corinthians, 3 John and other New Testament passages. We have to recognise that wherever people gather together there will be these tensions – even in the most up-to-date model of the church they will not be unknown.

But the third potential danger in the parochial model is the most important. As Stephen Platten says, 'Wherever the gospel is planted, the texture and make-up of the soil, the climate and the landscape will affect its growth'.[14] The Anglican parish church, or its Roman Catholic or Baptist equivalent, can too easily become part of the landscape and be so camouflaged by it that it is ultimately suffocated by its surroundings. The church ceases to be a missionary enterprise and becomes merely a local amenity like gas or electricity or the local post office. It becomes part of local life, which is expected to be on tap when it is needed and is otherwise ignored. Just as with electricity and the local post office, it is only really noticed when there is a breakdown in availability. Hence, we find an area which had appeared to be largely indifferent to a church building will react violently if there is any suggestion that it should be pulled down – and as a bishop I have to admit that I have the scars to prove it.

Much has rightly been said about 'missionary congregations' and the main principles have been spelt out by Robert Warren and others. Every part of congregational life is to be shot through with a missionary intent. Whether it is the occasional offices like funerals and marriages or the music used in worship, the place of the outsider has to be taken into consideration. As the 1980s' adage has it, 'A church that lives to itself, dies to itself'.

There is no doubt that most people who come to faith in the United Kingdom today do so through one of these incarnational communities, especially if they are looking outwards to serve and to save. It is easy to criticise and there is no doubt that part of the criticism is deserved, but it would be unwise to think that such local expressions of the Body of Christ will ever wither away entirely. Geography will always have a part to play: the danger is when acreage becomes the only criterion for ministry.

3. The *network* community

The 'homogeneous principle' suggests that ministry is best carried out among the like-minded: if you look like, think like and behave like the people you are ministering to you are more likely to win them for Christ. It is often associated with Donald McGavran who stated the principle after his study of missionary work in the 1950s: he proclaimed, 'People like to become Christians without crossing racial/linguistic/class/cultural barriers'.[15] I have to admit that for many years I resisted the idea: it seemed to be a negation of the whole glory of the Kingdom of God in which there are those 'from every tribe and language and people and nation'.[16] Certainly the implication of the principle seems to be that if you are reaching out only to those who are in a certain group, then you are not reaching out to the rest of humanity. Does this mean that the white-skinned do not reach out to the dark-skinned, or the educated to the ill-educated, or the poor to the rich? The idea that a local church would deliberately differen-tiate against some groups of people is almost a blasphemy. Yet it has to be admitted that many local churches do exclude those who are not the same as the congregation. They may not intend to do so but by the pattern of their church life this is what happens in practice: as we shall see, 'glass doors' shut out many.

We have to look at this again. The Bishop of Rochester, Michael Nazir-Ali, in a paper for the Church of England's Archbishop's Council,[17] asks the question: 'Some ways of gathering like-minded people, from a similar professional, cultural or even ethnic background, are undoubtedly effective in terms of outreach, but does a *church* always have to be heterogeneous, with a mix of ages, sexes and backgrounds?' He goes on to say, 'Different kinds of language, liturgy and music will be appropriate for different groups of people.'

I have no doubt that a church with a mix of people from different ages and from differing educational and ethnic backgrounds has a richer, more vibrant mix. Indeed, there is evidence that such churches are more likely to grow than those which are more homogeneous.[18]

Nevertheless, there is value in belonging to a network which has some of the same values as you do. Many people go to Spring Harvest or to Walsingham because the worship is to their taste, they find the teaching helpful and they enjoy the fellowship they find there. Through contact with those of a similar spiritual experience and outlook what Abbé Paul Couturier (1881–1953) called 'an invisible monastery' is formed: it has no building but there is a common desire to pray, to learn and to have fellowship. There are regulars who go to conferences year after year for the same reason. There are networks of Christian lawyers and Christian doctors. Those who belong are strengthened in their faith and their determination to walk with Christ is reinforced. There is little doubt that such networks will increase in numbers and significance. As we have seen in Chapter 4, as communication with others far away becomes easier the barriers of space become insignificant. It would be surprising if Christian WAP3 phone groups are not already forming somewhere in the world.

It is in this networking mode that new churches are arising. Church planting, seen as a *group* of people deliberately forming a new church, began in the 1980s, largely with the incarnational model of church in mind. But thinking has developed greatly over recent years: there is less emphasis on geography and more on 'creating new communities of Christian faith as part of the mission of God to express God's Kingdom in every geographic and cultural context'. The quotation comes from *Mission-shaped Church*, a report published in 2003 which was addressed to the Church of England. It was only in 1994 that a previous Anglican report looked at church planting: the viewpoint of *Breaking New Ground* was almost entirely to do with the local church planting churches elsewhere, mainly within its own parish boundaries. The difference between the two documents is startling. The 2003 report welcomes 'fresh expressions of church' wherever they are to be found. Even more surprising was the different reception given to the two reports. In 1994 the House of Bishops and the General

Synod were warm but guarded; in 2004 there was real enthusiasm as well as the inevitable questions for the much more radical report.

Cell churches are beginning to be assimilated into this wider view of church planting. Cell churches arise when local churches begin to see the small group as their focus rather than their congregation and to organise church life accordingly. When a cell church begins to draw in people from more than its locality, they are likely to be those of similar backgrounds and friendships and so their network church becomes a church plant.

We need also to look again at the place of what is sometimes rather dismissively called 'para-church'. It is an expression used to describe a body which is seen as an aid to the mainline Church, but which itself is not a 'proper' church. If we think that the only kind of church community is a local church in a certain area, then this is no doubt true. But if we expand the idea of church to include all groupings of Christian people who are seeking to do God's will, then what we now call 'para-church' becomes church. These bodies may well be more homogeneous than any local church but they fill a significant slot in the emerging Church. Not all colonies of heaven look the same.

I would therefore look for a growth of networks. Pete Ward contrasts 'liquid church' with the 'solid church' with its emphasis on the congregation gathered on Sunday. He enthuses,

> Liquid church would replace congregation with communication. The networked church would connect individuals, groups and organisations in a series of flows. Connection would rather be around hubs and could be made up of connecting nodes. A hub might be a retreat centre, a sports team, a music group, a record company, a Christian shop and so on. Connection to individuals and groups would involve sharing the life of Christ in a myriad of ways.[19]

Network communities seek to minister to a particular area of existence. Many which already exist, usually started by a group of enthusiasts or even a single person, play a significant role in the

Church. We would be wise to drop the belittling expression 'para-church' and embrace them as a full aspect of the Body of Christ.

The important characteristic of a network is that it is concerned to serve the world at large. What about the argument that a gathering of the like-minded can all too easily become self-satisfied and exclusive? The danger of introversion is certainly there and with it the death of any sense of mission. Because of this no Christian should ever belong *only* to a network. It is important that anyone who is involved in such a network should also be involved in another form of community, probably an incarna-tional one in their home locality. It is for this reason that Pete Ward's expectation that 'liquid' church will replace 'solid' church is unlikely to be fulfilled, and indeed it would be unfortunate if it did, for we shall not become mature Christians unless we are in community with those who are unlike us, who do not share our viewpoints and who challenge our assumptions. Networks built upon the homo-geneous principle are always potentially hazardous: any who venture in this direction need to remember David Bosch's stricture, 'This Protestant virus may no longer be tolerated as though it is the most natural thing in the world for a group of people to start their own church, which mirrors their foibles, fears and suspicions, nurtures their prejudices, and makes them feel comfortable and relaxed.'[20] Only a constant emphasis on mission can purify such a gathering.

4. The *focused* community

For a while I was the chairman of the Lee Abbey Council. Lee Abbey has three focused communities. There is one community of about eighty Christians running the well-known conference and retreat centre in North Devon. There is also a community of about thirty-five managing a hostel for 150 overseas students in London. In addition there is a much smaller community of seven divided between three houses in Urban Priority Areas in Blackburn, Birmingham and Bristol. Each community has its own focus, its own life and its own joys and difficulties. People may be a member of the community for as little as a few months or for several years. Some come from the United Kingdom, while many come from overseas.

By community is meant a group of people who have deliberately and publicly made promises that they will live in community, and respect, encourage and be open with each other. Nobody says that this is easy, but nearly all who have adopted this lifestyle see it as exhilarating and challenging – what someone called 'a crash course in growing up'.

The experience of Lee Abbey suggests that the community aspect is crucial. A research project asked departing guests from the Devon house after some days of teaching what had been most significant for them: the majority replied, 'The community'. Traditionally religious houses have been established to further education, to provide a spiritual haven for the weary or to engage in missionary work. These communities would also say that it is their experience of community which undergirds and sustains their work.

Many organisations are set up to achieve some Christian aim. Often an entrepreneur or a group will get together to meet some social or spiritual need. While not many lay as much stress as the religious orders and Lee Abbey on the importance of community, nearly all would emphasise the importance of teamwork, consultation and commitment.

One particular form of focused community which has been with us a very long time is the cathedral. By definition cathedrals have a community of canons to pray and work together. Unfortunately poor relationships within the cathedral close are not confined to the fictional world of Barchester and the Susan Howatch novels, and there have been far too many examples of such communities being dysfunctional. In part this is because of what a former dean of a cathedral called 'the satanic weight of the building' with its history and inevitable cost. Yet increasingly cathedrals are being seen as community buildings – not as being particularly denominationally defined, and also as places of the Spirit. Susan Hill speaks of cathedrals as 'the Still Point of the Turning World', and says that they are for those who 'do not reject the life of the spirit, and continue to search for that respite, that refuge, that solace'.[21]

The mixed experience of the cathedrals suggests that we would be unwise to be too idealistic about community. Being part of a community is not easy, but the more focused it is on the world outside the better. It is when a community becomes introspective and overconcerned with its own affairs that problems arise. The truth of the statement at the beginning of the chapter is once again borne out – 'Start with the mission and it is likely that the Church will be found'.

These focused communities should no longer be regarded merely as adjuncts to the 'mainstream' Church but as a genuine part of the Church and churches in their own right.

5. The *evangelistic* community

Of particular importance is the variety of focused community which sees itself as primarily evangelistic. This is no modern fad: its roots go back into the Middle Ages and even further back to the Celtic *perigrinati*. We may take our inspiration from the early friars 'who broke free from one of the most basic principles of traditional monasticism by abandoning the seclusion and enclosure of the cloister in order to engage in an active pastoral mission to the society of their time.'[22]

The twelfth and thirteenth centuries were a time of prosperity for much of Europe and the population was growing rapidly. Villages were expanding into towns and towns into cities. The usual diocesan pattern of the Church could not cope with these movements of people and so monks, especially the Dominicans and Franciscans began to minister in the new centres of population. They preached everywhere and begged for their daily bread. Taking Luke 10 seriously they went out with 'no purse, no bag, no sandals'. Their impact was enormous – so much so that those helped by them poured riches and possessions on to them and all too many of the mendicant friars gave way to temptation. It is a danger of success that is ever present.

There is a need for more communities for whom the evangelisation of the United Kingdom is their chief passion. They may be network communities or focused communities, but they will need to draw their resilience from being in community. By the very nature of their role evangelists are in an exposed position, for their task is 'to go where the church is not'.[23] There have been all too many examples of evangelists who have worked as lone rangers and fallen into the temptations which are inherent in such an approach.

In some ways the Springboard organisation, which has both practised and taught evangelism, in recent years has exemplified what is possible when a team of people work together to challenge, support and stimulate each other. Springboard is also illustrative of the need for and the importance of recognition by the wider Church: the fact that it was established by the Archbishop of Canterbury and had his backing has meant that it has been accepted and used by the Church much more readily than would otherwise have been the case.

More recently founded is The Order of Mission (TOM). It is a network community stemming from St Thomas Crookes in Sheffield which has learnt from the traditional religious orders in having a Superior and a Chapter of senior members, a three-year novitiate for those wishing to enter the Order, a Rule of Life for its members, and an outside Visitor who has the power to visit and require changes if necessary. It is too early to say how it will develop but its intention is that it should be global, and conversations have begun already with church leaders in several overseas countries.[24]

Another example is the Eden Project in Manchester which came into being as the result of the stimulus of the Soul Survivor organisation. Teams of mainly young people are involved in the life of the city and particularly the youth scene, and at considerable personal cost young Christians are serving the community of that great city.[25]

Why worry about what 'church' means?

It is all too easy to see thinking about what 'church' means as a esoteric fascination for insiders. We need also to remember 'Sharon', interviewed by David Hay and Kate Hunt. She said, 'I think they ought to do a church for beginners really . . .'

Why have I insisted that each of these five models should be called 'church'. There are at least five reasons for this extension to the normal meaning of the word as it is used in this country:

1. *By restricting the word 'church' only to what I have called incarnational communities we restrict the work of God.* In a world which is far more complex, far more interlocked and far more communicative than ever before, we cannot allow one model based on geography to dictate what we mean by church. I certainly do not disparage the incarnational community, nor do I expect it to disappear. Indeed, it may well be the main expression of church for a very long time into the future, for geography is still important to us. But we should not allow one model to swamp others or suggest that they are no more than assistants to the local. This is particularly important when we consider church planting. If we see church planting only in terms of producing more incarnational communities in more ecclesiastical buildings, then we will narrow God's purposes. Those seeking to plant churches need to think carefully about what sort of community it is that God is asking them to plant.

2. Down the centuries local incarnational communities have devised *support structures.* Some work better than others, but financial expertise, spiritual development and theological training are usually available through denominational structures. The other four models of community often do not have this support, and so are dependent almost entirely on their own resources. They may well be fiercely independent, but whether this is for their own good is questionable: inter-dependence is the most wholesome position for a Christian organisation.

3. Alongside support must go *accountability.* Far too many

Christian enterprises come to grief: some never get off the ground, some falter as soon as they are airborne, and some are too successful for their own good and cannot cope with growth. It is all too easy to see the same mistakes being made over and over again, with the resulting cost in terms of finance and time and, sometimes, scandal. If all communities are seen as fully church, then there needs to be a degree of accountability to the whole Christian community. Whether this is to be an extension of the present church structures for *episcope* or the evolving of some new pattern is yet uncertain. The need for it is all too evident. A glance at the *UK Christian Handbook* published by Christian Research shows the multiplicity of Christian organisations, most with their budget, their employees and their particular axe to grind. They overlap with each other; they get in each other's way; they waste an inordinate amount of Christian effort. The place of the Christian entrepreneur has a long and honourable history, but in an environment where the Christian Church is facing a completely new situation, it has to be questioned whether such a piecemeal approach can be justified.

The fierce independence of many non-incarnational communities shows a determination to fight for what they stand for. Since the mainstream Church dismisses them as, at best, no more than possibly useful adjuncts to its real work in the local churches, it is not surprising that these communities defend their position staunchly. If, however, they were to be seen as fully part of the Church of Christ, then they might well become more willing to listen to others, to consult before acting and to accept guidance when it is needed. Many of these groupings could learn from the traditional religious communities by having a respected Visitor from outside who can, at any time, come to encourage and criticise. Henry Venn's magnificent vision in 1846 of churches which were 'self-supporting, self-governing and self-propagating' was wonderful in helping the churches founded by missionaries to become strong and adult. But it is not sufficient, for all churches are part of the Church Catholic and need nourishment from outside.

4. The need for *intercommunication and common research*. The lack of any overall guidance of research and the appropriate communication of the results to the Christian community has meant that many churches have repeatedly tried methods which others have shown to be unsuccessful, simply because they were unaware of the experience of others. For example the large survey carried out by Christian Research at the end of 2003 appears to show *that none of the following help a local church to grow:*

cell groups	more Eucharistic services
a link with a church school	having special evangelistic events
an attractive church building	a well-educated congregation
provision for young people	church planting.[26]

But the survey was done on the initiative of the Central North Division of the Salvation Army. Should it have been left to them? I know myself the difficulty in getting backing for proper research, because there is no body which has oversight of research.[27] The Christian churches in this country could do much to help their work if they were able together to both finance research and ensure that the findings were properly disseminated. The importance of this cannot be overestimated. If the rather startling statements made above are correct, then many churches have spent endless hours and much money chasing up blind alleys. According to the same survey they would have been better employed seeking to grow their churches through:

ensuring visionary leadership	giving a warm welcome to newcomers
keeping leaders for at least seven years	giving consecutive exposition of the Bible
having regular nurture courses	having an ethnic mix in the congregation
concentrating on the elderly and parents with toddlers.	

The need for sound, authoritative and widely accepted research could not be more clearly stated.

5. There is a need for *recognition* by the wider Church. A good example is the Springboard initiative which I have already mentioned: the fact that it was established by the Archbishop of Canterbury and seen to be responsible to him meant that it was accepted far more quickly and was far more successful in its work than would have been the case if it had been an organisation without recognition. This is particularly the case for evangelistic communities. They work at the edge and need to be seen to have acceptance by the wider Church: the establishing of the College of Evangelists by the Church of England has gone some way to remedy the situation, but there is always the need for constant dialogue between those who are in community and the mainstream of the Church.

Martyn Atkins puts it succinctly, 'Second millennium denominationalism will become Third millennium monasticism'.[28] The centrality of the Christian community, in one or other of the various forms suggested above, is crucial to the Christian mission. As Archbishop Rowan Williams says, church is 'the community that happens when people meet the living Christ'. That should not be restricted to only one form of community, however hoary with history it may be.

CHAPTER 8

Leading over the Hurdles

Post-modern leadership

Fortunately there are now some excellent books on leading a church into the brave new world of the twenty-first century. Out of the welter of possibilities I and others have found the following particularly useful:

> Peter Drucker, *Managing the non-profit organisation* (Harper, 1990)
>
> Chris Edmondson, *Fit to Lead* (DLT, 2002)
>
> John Finney, *Understanding Leadership* (DLT, 1989)
>
> Robin Greenwood, *Transforming Priesthood* (SPCK, 1994)
>
> Henri Nouwen, *Creative Ministry* (Image/Doubleday, 1978)
>
> Derek Tidball, *Builders and Fools: leadership the bible way* (IVP, 1999)

However, there is one area which is all too often missed in books about leadership. Long ago I came across this dictum, 'Operate in the negative force field'. By this the business guru meant, 'Don't just look at what you need to reinforce, but also look at what is holding you back'. The largest airliner can rev its engines until everyone around is deafened but it will not move an inch unless someone takes away the chocks.

I have found this invaluable advice. In pastoral situations it means that I should try to talk as much with those who disagree with me as with those who support me. It means we should face objections before proposing some course of action rather than being bewildered when they are fired at us later.

It also resonates with the work of evangelism. If we are not careful, it can seem as though we begin by speaking to people about the gospel: when they do not listen, we start shouting at them; and when they still do not listen we end up shrieking at them. There is too much OTT evangelism which deafens but does not penetrate.

A much more sensible approach is to see what the barriers to faith are. What are the chocks which prevent the mission of the Church going forward?

We do so, not just so that our evangelism may be more effective, but to make it easier for Christ to come into people's lives. Isaiah speaks of the need to clear away the obstacles so that, in the words of Psalm 24:7, 'the King of glory may come in':

> 'In the wilderness prepare the way of the Lord,
> make straight in the desert a highway for our God.
> Every valley shall be lifted up,
> and every mountain and hill be made low . . .
> and the rough places a plain.
> Then the glory of the Lord shall be revealed
> and all people shall see it together . . .'[1]

Jesus called a man-made obstruction a *skandalon* – something which prevents people coming to faith. One of his severest condemnations is directed at anyone who puts a barrier in front of 'one of these little ones': it would 'be better for you if a great millstone were hung around your neck and you were thrown into the sea'.[2]

Some barriers come from the society in which we live and the culture which we inhabit – in African or Indian societies faith in the spiritual is in some ways easier than it is in Europe or Australasia. We shall look at three of these cultural *skandalon* later in the chapter.

But we do not have only to look outside the Church: there are *skandalon* inside.

Glass doors

Why do we stop people coming to church?

I was once part of a team of church leaders invited by an English diocese to look at its workings and produce a report. Each of us was given a section of diocesan life to examine during the four weeks of the survey. One of the visitors was the wife of an arch-deacon from Botswana. She was allotted 'Youth Work'. At the end of the visit we all sat down and catalogued our findings: most of us had written many pages. She just wrote one sentence on a sheet of A4: 'Young People: why do you stop them coming?'

It turned the whole matter on its head. Instead of worrying, 'How do we get young people to come to church?', she made us think of what we were doing which prevented them from coming. We looked at the church and our failings rather than railing at the young people who seemed disinterested and awkward.

We are now familiar with the idea of 'glass ceilings' – those unseen but very real obstacles which prevent the 'excluded' rising above a certain level in an organisation. This is particularly true of women and coloured people. Even now there is only one chair-*woman* of any of the top 100 British companies, and hardly a black face in the officers' mess of any crack British regiment.

Churches need to ask themselves if they have any 'glass doors'. They cannot be seen but they shut people out. Many medieval churches have heavy oak doors studded with nails: they are formidable indeed and shout, 'Keep out!' But more insidious and more important are the unseen barriers which shut people out of worship.

To take an example. A church has its main service at 10 a.m. on a Sunday morning. By that very action its glass door excludes:

- everyone who has to work on a Sunday (about 30 per cent of the population)
- all children of divorcees for whom Sunday is the day

127

when they have to see their 'other' parent – and also
those parents looking after their offspring

- those young people for whom Sunday is the only day on
which they can play sport competitively – if you want to
be a member of the football team you play on a Sunday.

And, while not making it impossible, it is difficult for:

- those Christians from non-Christian families for whom
Sunday is the main day for shopping[3]
- those for whom Sunday is the only day for a lie-in and for
whom getting the children organised for church means
a very early start.

Each community will add its own local obstacles. In some places
Sunday is the day when Football League matches take place. In
tourist resorts it is often the busiest day of the week. Some towns
are dominated by a factory which requires shift work.

But that is not all – each church provides its own obstacle course
by the nature of the service which is being held. A communion
service will seem to be exclusively for 'insiders' and a 'Family
Service' will seem to diminish those who do not have families.

Further, the very style of the service excludes. This is inevitable,
but it is important to be aware of who is shut out. Broadly speaking a cheerful charismatic service will alienate those who dislike
that style (and who do not know the songs), and may not meet the
needs of those who are going through a time of personal suffering.
On the other hand, a more traditional service excludes children
(because they shuffle and squeak from boredom) as well as the
more exuberantly inclined (because they shuffle and squeak with
frustration). A meditative service will shut out those whose personality finds silence unhelpful, while unending Taizé verses have
no appeal for others. A service full of bonhomie discriminates
against the loner and those who are shy.[4]

In some areas there are social barriers. However much it may be
denied, one church may really be a place where only the successful and the articulate feel comfortable, while another is geared

totally towards the white highlanders who feel threatened by an influx of immigrants. In some village communities, newcomers may wrest the church away from the long-established members, or the latter may cling desperately to control. I have even encountered a church whose ministry is still hampered by the expectation that the masters and mistresses will come to the morning service while the servants come in the evening.

All of these obstacles are 'glass doors' – you cannot see them but they are as impenetrable as those heavy medieval doors. If evangelism is seen in part in terms of churchgoing, it is a sobering thought that such a high proportion of the population cannot come to the local church's main 'shop window'. Deeper than that, we have to realise that many are kept away from the worship of God, not through any fault of their own, but simply because of contemporary lifestyles and the culture of the local church.

After a discussion about glass doors, I often ask church committees, 'What proportion of the people in your community are prevented from coming to your main service because of the glass doors?' The answer is always 'over half' – one church was honest to admit that 89 per cent of local people could not come.

What is the answer? Recent statistics point us in a helpful direction. While the number of people coming to church on a Sunday has been in decline, the number coming to church on a weekday has been increasing. The same research shows that many of those coming on weekdays never come on a Sunday: some come on a weekday because they are excluded from Sunday by one of the glass doors; some come because they prefer the sort of service which is on offer – often quieter, less crowded, more friendly.

One vicar went to the local primary school head and asked, 'Why do so few children come to church on a Sunday morning?' She replied, 'Because you have your service at one of the hardest times in the week for any child to come.' As a result he began a service on Monday afternoons at 4 p.m.: nearly all children these days are picked up from school by an adult,[5] and so, after school was over, they came to church, had refreshments and then a communion service. I asked him, 'Why do you have communion? Very few are confirmed, so why not have some sort of family service?' He replied, 'You have got it wrong: this is not a half-way house into the Sunday morning service – this is their church.' Talking to the many adults who were later confirmed, I found out he was right: very few had ever been to church on a Sunday and nearly half of them worked on a Sunday. Monday afternoon had become their time for 'church' and they depended on it for their worship, their teaching and their fellowship. The vicar led a service which was different but linked with Sunday worship, and again he had got it right for a weekday service should not be a pale phantasm trying to replicate the Sunday worship. After a few years the numbers at the Monday service rivalled the regular Sunday morning service.

These innovations began in that church as a result of some simple questions. It is not difficult for a church to learn what people's motivations are through some easy research – just ask them.

When such a thing is suggested it is always objected, 'This will split the church'. Behind the grumble lies the antiquated cliché, 'All the Lord's people round the Lord's table on the Lord's day'. It is a slogan harking back to the beginnings of the Parish Communion Movement in the 1950s and it needs to die. The idea of the Great Gathering of the faithful in one magnificent Sunday service was always suspect. After half a century of sociological and ecclesiastical change it is a sacred cow which prevents rather than encourages progress: it needs to be slaughtered.

It is also objected that Sunday is the 'right' time to worship, and worship at any other time is somehow less worthy. While it is of course true that from the earliest days worship has been held on the day of the resurrection,[6] there seems no genuine reason except tradition for it to be restricted to Sunday. Genesis 1 emphasises that the seventh day should be a day of rest – it says nothing about worship. Until 1993 the Church had a stranglehold on Sunday morning, enforced by the Sunday Trading legislation. This privileged position has been swept away, and the Church must seek to invade the whole week and not be shut into a ghetto from the past. Personally I think that the change of pace dictated by having one day different from the other six made for a healthier society but we can no longer try to recreate the past.

A missionary church will seek to provide worship for as wide a spectrum of people and spiritual needs as possible.

Confronting the perception of religion in modern culture

We can do something about glass doors within the church, but more difficult is the dark fog created by contemporary culture which prevents many from seeing the light.

There are the obvious and age-long barricades to faith such as materialism, hedonism, self-centredness and the like. But there are three other barriers which are less readily seen and which are becoming more and more persistent in people's minds.

The first is that the Church is often seen as tough on those in need. Whether it is divorcees trying to get married, the terminally ill trying to die, homosexuals trying to live out their lifestyle, women trying to be upwardly mobile, couples trying to have babies or the careless trying to stop having babies, we are seen as unsympathetic and tough. In a very sentimental age TV thrusts in our face the man dying in agony, the raped girl with an unwanted child, the 'Christian leader' who says that women should be kept in the kitchen and the bishop who says that fertility experiments should be stopped. However personally sympathetic and kind we may be, our Christian principles are seen as making us hard and censorious and unable to deal adequately with the rugged realities of human existence.

I wish I knew the answer to this dilemma. The Bible sees sin as sin, and we cannot but say as much. At the same time these Christian standards mean that many are refusing to listen to the good news which we bring. I wish there was an easy answer, but I fear there is none outside the vulnerability of the cross. There are two things we can do: one is to make sure that the standards we seek to maintain really are the standards of the Scriptures rather than our own prejudices, and the other is to learn humility.

Second, allied to this is the bad press which religion as a whole is having. Few news programmes today do not mention Islamic terrorists, in the same way that a few years ago they talked about Catholic and Protestant gunmen in Northern Ireland. Inter-faith conflict seems to be everywhere – in India between Muslim and Hindu; in Pakistan between Sunni and Shia Muslims; in Indonesia, Sudan and Nigeria between Muslims and Christians; and above all the Muslim/Jewish strife in Israel. They all give 'religion' a bad name. The horror of 9/11 has thrust the dangers of religiously inspired venom into everyone's consciousness. In the twentieth century by far the greatest number of people died as a result of the actions of atheistic governments under Stalin, Hitler, Pol Pot, Mao and the depressing rest. In the twenty-first century so far we have seen avowedly religious regimes taking over the baton.[7] It is a depressing reality.[8]

Third, in an age which seems to have no standards and yet is intensely judgemental, the Church has given all-too-much ammunition to those who have always claimed 'they are all a bunch of hypocrites'. The downfall of the tele-evangelists in the US rocked that particular religious milieu. The continuing revelations about gross sins perpetrated by priests and nuns in the Roman Catholic Church have changed the public mood. A Roman Catholic priest who is a friend of mine went over to Dublin wearing his clerical clothing: he said he was spat at once and shouted at twice on his journey by public transport from the airport to where he was staying. Nor can we say that this only affects high-profile evangelists and Catholic priests: it makes all Christian leaders suspect, just as imams are affected by the prevalent Islamaphobia. It is not surprising that in polls about the public estimation of significant figures in the community, when people were asked, 'Whom in the community do you trust?' the local vicar has slid from second place to near the bottom. It does not make it easier for us to get our message over to people. It may suggest that we need to be more illustrative of the love of God.

I include these three 'religious' barriers because we would be foolish not to recognise that we paddle against the stream. It may make the Church a little less defensive of its 'rights', a little more prepared to listen as well as to talk, a little more prepared to dress in sackcloth and ashes rather than take the mantle of power. We may even need to accept that some scorn us and we can make no reply, for as Archdeacon Paley said, 'Who can refute a sneer?'[9] Perhaps it may even make us more like our Saviour who was reviled and falsely accused. It may even make us rely more upon the Holy Spirit rather than our carefully engineered schemes and programmes.

. . . and one (nearly) non-existent barrier

Clergy often suppose that churchgoers find church services are a barrier to discipleship. They are therefore tempted to tinker with the services by seeking to amuse as well as to pray and to provide the latest liturgical fad or the song from the most recent CD. One of the largest surveys of church opinion ever carried out was the Church Life Survey in 2001. It asked the opinions of over 100,000 churchgoers from more than ten denominations. It found that:

> well under half of the members of the congregation *ever* found services boring or frustrating

> the great majority found that the services were inspirational and conveyed a sense of the presence of God

> only 4% disagreed with the statement that 'the preaching in the local church is usually very helpful to me in my everyday life'.[10]

I personally find this hard to believe – but then I am a clergyman! I do think, however, that it suggests that altering the services is unlikely to bring in the Kingdom, and the lust to meddle with liturgy is often best resisted. Sensible changes should, of course, be made but extravagant hopes that the results will be startling are best repressed.

This chapter is inevitably somewhat downbeat, for it deliberately sets out to deal with problems. But truth can be the beginning of wisdom.

The new vicar of a mining community said he had 'tried all the handbooks suggested' and at the end of much effort the congregation had halved. He had previously been involved with mission in Africa and decided to try the cross-cultural models he had used overseas to try to understand the reaction of people within his community. He studied at Ph.D. level all the areas of resistance. It gave him a deep insight into the thinking of people and a more empathetic approach. After the disappointments of following what the bandwagons claimed was the certain way to get your church to grow, he found 'a new church has grown up in the village, built, not on overt evangelism, but on pastoral care of the bereaved, a warmth of welcome to the church, Alpha courses, and (amazingly) said Book of Common Prayer worship'.[11]

By all means accentuate the positive, but also identify the negative.

CHAPTER 9

Ritual and Relationship

The problem

The evangelist Ravi Zacharias has asked a key question for the twenty-first century:

> How do you reach a generation that listens with its eyes and thinks with its feelings?

We have examined the impact of post-modernism, and come to suspect that *mysterion* may have at least as much to say to today's culture as the wordiness of *kerugma* or *evangelion*. We have looked at the development of the evangelistic message and realised that an Athenian gospel spread in the market-place is going to be very different from an Antiochan sermon preached from the pulpit.

Zacharias' question is not answered by a flurry of words but by a different approach which is likely to be non-verbal, human in its acceptance of non-rationality and emotion, able to walk alongside and understand. We have also found that it is the Holy Spirit who works in the area of *mysterion*, and so we need to examine his work in our midst.

Mysterion in practice

We have found in Chapter 7 that various styles of community in the church will enshrine the gospel. All research has shown that nearly everyone coming to faith enters through the gateway of the church – whether the church becomes visible to them as a friend, a nurture group, the meeting of a social need or a sacred space. In other words, people are converted to the church before being converted to Jesus Christ.

We shall look at four areas[1] where mysterion is in operation:

relationships
ritual
the Charismatic
eschatology.

Relationships

Writing about 150 AD a Christian could say with justifiable pride: 'Beauty of life causes strangers to join our ranks . . . we do not talk about great things; we live them.'[2]

A young friend of the renowned biblical scholar Origen (185–254) was called Gregory. Day after day the great man talked with him, and later Gregory wrote, 'he possessed a rare combination of a certain sweet grace and persuasiveness'. It was not so much the intellectual argument of Origen that brought Gregory to full commitment to Christ as 'the argument of a kind and affectionate disposition'.[3]

Again and again a relationship with a Christian leads to a relationship with Christ. In the *Finding Faith Today* research more than 80 per cent of those who had come to faith said that the main factor in bringing them to faith was a relationship. Interestingly, only a quarter of these people said that it was a friendship with just one person: *for most it was a friendship with a group of people –* they had begun to be at ease in a Christian milieu and hence had become receptive to the beliefs of the others.[4]

Thus, for most people the corporate life of the church is a vital element in the process of becoming a Christian. This in turn indicates that any form of evangelism which downplays or ignores the church is likely to be of limited effect. All parts of the New Testament suggest the same since the need for love, unity and forbearance is stressed repeatedly. The church should be aware of visitors and welcome them and show respect. Long before 'seeker services', Paul, in his discussion on the public use of tongues, required that worship should 'build up' the outsider: he pointed out that the danger lay in the fact that 'the outsider does not know what you are saying' and so was bewildered (see 1 Cor. 14:16–19).

The *Finding Faith Today* research also gives a pointer as to what it is in Christians which outsiders find important. Again and again respondents mentioned *integrity*: as one said, 'My friend seemed so "at one" with herself; she seemed to radiate, even through times of trouble'. When Christians show a basic trustworthiness and honesty in their dealings with people they are making a good witness. It is significant that the root of the word 'holy' is the Anglo-Saxon word *hal* which means 'whole' and is also the root of 'health' and 'wholesomeness'. The New Testament word *sozo* can mean 'to save' or 'to make whole' and refer to either being saved from sin or cured from illness.

In an age where so many are 'walking wounded' such integrity of personality is enormously powerful in helping others to wholeness in Christ. In a post-modern age it speaks of God more persuasively than words, for it is part of the *mysterion* of the Spirit.

At the same time Christians should not assume that friendships lead automatically to faith. Modern relationships are exceedingly important, but they are also transient: a marriage, cohabitation or friendship may flourish only for a time, until a new interest beckons. The same can be true of faith itself – so often people can view their 'religious phase' as no more than a passing fascination: 'been to Alpha, had the experience, got the T-shirt, finished'.

Ritual

From his evangelical background Canon Robert Warren is able to say, 'The future of worship belongs to the catholic tradition'. Post-moderns like sacraments and icons and, since they find verbal explanations constricting, they prefer the use of symbols to represent ideas; furthermore, they wish to invest a symbol with their own meaning rather than have it imposed on them by an authority figure.

This is seen in the extreme in the New Age. Its ideas may be fuzzy and incoherent, but its *things* which meaning: crystals, amulets, body piercing all have significance. Places like

Glastonbury are more than dots on the map. The occult in its various forms is ritualistic to a degree.

But this growth of ritual spreads far beyond the specifically New Age environment. It can be particularly seen in the secular treatment of death. In a return to pre-Christian practices the dead are increasingly buried with things they valued placed beside their body; roadside shrines are set up to mark a fatal accident; people visit graveyards not just to tidy a grave but to talk to those buried there.

The Christian Church has always had its rituals. These vary from the respectability of the scriptural sacraments through pilgrimages to preposterous weeping madonnas and cartwheeling suns. The Bible is extraordinarily physical and the worship of the Psalms encourages clapping, dancing and the use of all kinds of musical instrument! The laying on of hands with prayer is a sort of all-purpose sacramental sign. Its original meaning was probably as a sign of identification, as is illustrated by the rituals surrounding the scapegoat banished into the wilderness bearing the sins of the people:[5] it also came to be used as a sign for healing, for commissioning, for the reception of the Holy Spirit and for blessing. While the Church has too often forgotten the ministry of healing, and formalised the other uses into ordination, confirmation and 'giving the blessing', the power of the laying on of hands with prayer is still there, as is witnessed in many a 'time of ministry' in more charismatic churches.

When we think of ritual, we too easily confine the idea to solemn processions and clouds of incense. Indeed, the aversion of many to the whole idea stems from a wish for simplicity and, above all, from a fear that the reality and unadorned claims of the Word will be lost among ritualistic trappings. The 'stripping of the altars' at the Reformation had exactly this purpose: it was a theological statement as well as a desire for relief from the complexities of Catholic worship and an aesthetic hunger for simplicity. However, we may today have to come to terms with a culture in which the Word is not clearly perceived except through ritual. The verbal and cerebral has lost its potency and at the same time the experiential and mysterious affects people more deeply than before.

A contemporary indication of this love of the concrete as opposed to the theoretical is the current cult of the orange. As I mentioned briefly in Chapter 3, in many English churches the Christingle service has taken over from Harvest as the best-attended service of the year. It is a service which has more than a touch of *mysterion*, with the shadows of a December day, the expectation of the coming Christmas, and the orange and its attachments conveying a 'mystic meaning'. Yet it only began in 1968 as an inspired borrowing by the Children's Society of an old Moravian tradition.[6]

The Christingle illustrates an important aspect of ritual for the service has an element of playfulness to which both adults and children respond. Victor Turner describes play as a 'kind of dialectical dancing partner of ritual'.[7] Richard Schechner speaks of rituals as 'antistructural, creative, often carnivalesque and play-ful'.[8] When thinking of ritual we need to imagine South Americans dancing through the streets at a religious festival as well as solemn evensong. Indeed, it is when ritual loses this element of gaiety that pomposity and excessive precision creep in: it is never meant to be taken too seriously. Turner links it with the two hemispheres of the brain, where the right side sees the impact of ritual as being beyond verbal explanation, while the left side tries inadequately to describe and make sense of the 'ecstatic'. Therefore, ritual which is too cerebral loses the whisper of wonder but if it loses contact with the rational it descends into magic, where it is supposed that the performance of certain actions are bound to lead to predictable consequences.

It is for this reason that the innovative and creative use of things which can become sacramental to the worshippers needs to be seen in our churches. In some ways the new liturgies of Common Worship encourage this, but sadly only through its rubrics: the overall impression is of an avalanche of words which buries the worshipper. Nevertheless, we should not disparage a snowball that one individual can start rolling: just as the Christingle service was the initiative of someone in the Children's Society, so the Harvest Festival service was created by the eccentric Robert Hawker in the tiny village of Morwenstow in Cornwall in 1843,[9] the Parish Communion movement which has become the mainstay of Anglican worship began as the result of the drive of Ernie Southcott and a few friends, and nurture courses were developed by individuals trying to meet a need in their churches.

Creativity in the Spirit can have reverberations which echo far from its starting point.

The charismatic

This section can be seen as flowing on from the last, for the use of things and actions are obvious in charismatic practice while the preaching and singing tend to be less dependent upon the cerebral. Ritual is more acceptable and in charismatic evangelical churches I have been asked to perform ceremonies which would be regarded as exclusively catholic, including asperging the congregation with water from the font and swinging the thurible so that the incense rises in clouds. It can be argued that the right and left sides of the brain are kept in better balance among the charismatics than in much of Christian worship.

It is estimated that 27 per cent of Christians worldwide are from the charismatic/pentecostal stream. It is certainly reasonable to maintain that this spirituality combines many of the factors which appeal to the post-modern world. Margaret Paloma, a sociologist who has for many years researched the charismatic movement and the phenomena associated with it, says, 'The pentecostal/ charismatic approach to Christianity is a curious combination of premodern, modern and post-modern elements that transcend both national and denominational boundaries.'[10] She claims that those involved in the charismatic movement are engaged in a form of mysticism, but one which is more involved with the everyday world than the traditional mystical withdrawal from the world. Thus, she calls her study of the happenings at Toronto *Main Street Mystics*[11] because it was open to all. There are certainly similarities between the spiritualities which lie behind mysticism and those that undergird the charismatic. Pentecostalism also has its places of pilgrimage – Sunderland, Pensacola, Toronto, Portland, Pretoria in the recent past – to which people come in their thousands. Just as among those who go on pilgrimage to Lourdes and Compostela, some go seeking God while others seek for wonders and perhaps the majority go with the normal confused human motivations. Further, in the whole English-speaking charismatic world from New Zealand to Britain there is an extraordinary capacity for a single idea to become part of the thinking of millions: thus the Kansas prophets were succeeded by Power Healing, which was followed by Toronto . . . It is not dissimilar from the spiritual world of the past where a single book like Gregory's *Dialogues* published in 593, which promoted the work of Benedict and his monastic Rule, became so influential that the Rule was adopted throughout the Latin-speaking world, changing the face of the Church until the present day.

The place of play is evident in much of what happens in charismatic gatherings. Laughter, movement, gaiety, excitement are present. A sense of anticipation, of 'I wonder what is going to happen next', is often prevalent. The unusual shaking, jerking and stamping which was frequently witnessed at Toronto was described by one of its leaders as 'God playing with his kids'. It is intriguing that when similar manifestations were seen two hundred years earlier in camp meetings on the western frontier of the expanding United States, a similar sense of release, playfulness and wellbeing were experienced.[12]

Further, as in ritual, charismatic mysticism instinctively wishes to be in company with others. Just as a ritual procession of one person is unimpressive, so a charismatic yearns to be with the like minded. In the three parables in Luke 15, when that which was lost was found we are told that those rejoicing gathered their friends together to celebrate with them: in the same way, contemporary people prefer to be joyous together. The community is important.

It has to be admitted that charismatic ritual can become as formalised as high mass in a cathedral. There is always a desire to avoid risk and to seek to control the work of the Holy Spirit. The laying on of hands becomes an all-too-predictable rite of ordination where it is not expected that the Holy Spirit will do anything outside the rubrics of the ordinal. A pentecostal leader lamented that 'in our churches we have pushed out the Holy Spirit by predictability'. At many charismatic gatherings the music, the worship, the preaching are carefully scripted and no room is given for the unexpected, the spontaneous and the extemporaneous.

Eschatology

St Augustine of Hippo came across people who were ignoring their Bible and trying to predict the future:

> In vain therefore do we try to reckon and set limits to the years that remain to this world, when we hear from the Mouth of Truth that it is not ours to know this. Yet some have said that 400, some 500, others even a thousand years must be reached between the Lord's ascension and his last coming.

In respectable circles the Christian Church in the West has tended to avoid discussion of eschatology and 'the Last Things' – heaven and hell, the return of Christ, judgement and the apocalyptic. This avoidance is partly because of a distaste for the whole subject and partly because of the sort of foolishness that Augustine encountered fourteen hundred years ago and which is all too alive today.

Yet, we live in an age fascinated by the subject. Last century was dominated, on the one hand, by an attempt to establish the Triumph of Socialism when all power would wither away and human beings would finally be free and, on the other, by a struggle to found the Reich that would last for a thousand years. These secular beliefs certainly fit the *American Encyclopedia of Religion*'s definition that millenarianism 'is a belief that the end of the world is at hand and that, in its wake, will appear a New World, inexhaustibly fertile, harmonious, sanctified and just'.[13] In its theoretical models capitalism shares the same utopianism, seeking a society where all are free to pursue their own goals and yet all are provided for. Lesslie Newbigin saw them both as 'the twin products of the apostasy of the European intellectuals of the eighteenth century',[14] and called communism 'Capitalism's rebellious twin sister'. The difference between the two is that communism pursues equality at the cost of freedom while capitalism pursues freedom at the cost of equality.

Scientifically we are fascinated by our own demise. Programme after programme and book after book proclaim that the human race will die by freezing or frying, by choking on its own wastes, by famine or by gluttony or overwhelmed by some superbug. Even when cosmologists say that the sun will engulf the earth in umpteen million years, it sends a frisson down our spine.

But this is nothing to the rampant predictions of the New Age. Aquarius is in the ascendant and, as a result, the possibilities for prophecy and predictions seem endless. From George Adamski's supposed encounter with a flying saucer in the 1950s to the latest on the best-seller list, there have been a myriad of ideas. Some supposedly stem from aliens, some from human prophets like the Chippewa medium man Sun Bear, some from astrological computation, some from spirit guides, some from Gnostic forms of hidden wisdom.

Are we right to play down the eschatalogical which is so conspicuous a part of so much of our biblical heritage? We cannot write off those Christians to whom this is a mainspring of their faith along with Hal Lindsey and his fantastical predictions. As David Bosch says:

> It would not do simply to label all millenarians as crackpots. The validity of their views lies in the anger and protest they voice against the complacency of the main Christian body, and against an understanding of history as a crisscrossing of chance impulses, and an accidental flow of bodies tumbling over the cataract of time to their destruction.[15]

Christian eschatology is not vague theories about the last days, it is an account of God's action in history, visible in the Old

Testament and continued into our present situation. The details of the new heaven and the new earth are not given and should not concern us, but the sense of the ongoing purposeful advance of the Kingdom should. It may be as hidden as the working of yeast in a lump of dough[16] but it transforms everything.

The drama of salvation is far more than the conversion of the individual or the upbuilding of the Church. It is part of a cosmic contest. As Walter Brueggemann says, 'there really is a massive, albeit hidden struggle for the shape, governance and future of the world'.[17] The New Testament vision of the 'principalities and powers' working behind the world we see introduces the whole field of spiritual conflict and the need to resist and to overcome. When we privatise our religion and make it just an I-Thou relationship between me and my Maker we challenge nothing, and that is just how the principalities and powers like it to be.

If we have the Scriptures which manifestly include this element and we do not explain it nor invite people to make it part of their experience, then there will be those who find in the Bible a hidden Code or who fly away on the most fanciful suppositions of millenarianism. We may be emptying the faith of mystery by insisting that all of our preaching and teaching should be relevant to this present time, forgetting that people are also drawn to speculate about the future and the end of all things. They need to be assured that all things are to be part of 'a plan for the fullness of time, to gather up all things in him [Christ], things in heaven and things on earth'.[18]

Thomas Merton describes the Christian as a watcher, looking and waiting:

> We are exiles in the far end of solitude, living as listeners, with hearts attending to the skies we cannot understand, waiting upon the first far drums of Christ the Conqueror, planted like sentinels upon the world's frontier.

CHAPTER 10

The Emerging Church

From the matrix of our culture we have begun to perceive the outline of a new form of Church emerging. If this book is right, then the Church:

(a) will be fully Trinitarian in its thinking about Christian initiation and our life in God. In particular, it will not rely so much on words and more on the work of the Holy Spirit in that imprecise but wonder-filled *mysterion* which touches at the deepest levels.

(b) will finally put behind it forms of evangelism which are centred upon formulae and over-dependence upon the outside expert.

(c) will recognise that the gospel as preached to the Athenians which surround us may be very different and more diverse in content than that with which the church people at Antioch are familiar.

(d) will expand beyond the incarnational model which we know so well into new patterns that we are only now beginning to discern. The local church in its parish will remain but there will be many other forms of being church, often taking their inspiration from the monastic orders of Christian history.

(e) will give *mysterion* its full place by the acceptance by the whole Church of the ritualistic and the charismatic and the playful rather than confining them to certain traditions. We should not be frightened just because we cannot explain something in words.

That is all very well. But how do we move from here to there?

First of all we need to recognise how much has already been done. We looked in Chapters 3 and 4 at the enormous change which has come over evangelism during the last twenty years although very few have been conscious of it. In the last ten years church planting has widened its horizons. *Mission-shaped Church* shows that it no longer thinks just in terms of merely planting from one geographical area to another, but suggests a wide variety of different patterns, which both demand a more inclusive view of what we mean by 'church' and a willingness to accept the experimental and entrepreneurial. The traditions in the Church now learn from each other and a less party-minded Church is developing, despite some who stay noisily in the old trenches. The importance of relationships and community has been grasped by many: even charismatic phenomena no longer produce the same shocked reaction they once did. The Church is more ready than ever to recognise that change is inevitable, and is remarkably willing to accept it: indeed, many are excited by the possibility and look forward with eagerness as well as apprehension.

There are two other things which are going to have to change. The first is the way we learn within the Church, and the second is our understanding of holiness.

Learning: back to the New Testament

The non-clerical Church

The Roman Catholic Church in Ireland has only one seminary still open. In 2003 only thirteen new seminarians began training at Maynooth, yet Ireland used to produce priests in their tens of thousands and exported them to every part of the globe. The situation in the Roman Catholic Church in Europe, North America and many other parts of the world is critical: men are no longer coming forward for the priesthood. Though the situation is not as dire in other denominations, it is similar and nearly all have a declining number of stipendiary teachers and preachers.

There are two possible reactions: one is to wring our hands and launch a recruitment campaign. This implies that the professional is essential, and that without him or her nothing can happen. But this is already meaning that fewer and fewer clergy are having to do more and more. The result is stress, inefficiency and a declining sense of fulfilment: Roman Catholic priests speak of their guilt as they rush from mass to mass without time to care for people, while Protestant clergy say they are so tied to sermons and administration they have little time to pray. Too many spiral into breakdown and burnout.

The alternative is to ask the question, 'Perhaps God is behind it?' Maybe God is no longer calling as many to the 'ordained ministry' as heretofore? Perhaps God wants a less clericalised, less hierarchically structured Church? In Chapter 2 we saw that a Church concentrating on the *kerugma* idolised the teacher, and a Church proclaiming *evangelion* revered the preacher. During the long history of the Church the teachers/preachers came to be seen as the leaders of the Church and evolved into a different caste, with special clothes and a multiplicity of possible titles. Ecclesiastical power steadily flowed in that direction until Catholicism exalted the pope as the supreme Teacher and Protestantism built the Preacher an imposing pulpit six feet above contradiction. Things are changing. Roman Catholics may hold the papacy in high esteem, but they make up their own minds about such matters as birth control and relationships with other Christians. Protestants do not flock in such numbers to hear the famous Dr X expound the Word in hour-long sermons. The authority figures look less intimidating. Their pedestals are cracked.

The laity have come of age and the Church must adapt to the new situation. Talk of shepherds and flock, of leaders and led, no longer has reality. The Church still needs leadership but even good modern business practice shows that this does not necessarily mean hierarchy. If the Church relies on a diminishing number of clergy and ministers, it will wither into insignificance. Helping lay people to be Christians in the world is one of the greatest tasks of the contemporary Church.

Unfortunately, since the clergy have been seen as the most prestigious members of the Church, it has been all too common for lay people who seek for training to be trained as though they were to be clergy. And nearly all clergy have been trained in a modernist setting. Lay people seeking to be trained are turned into 'students': it undermines their self-confidence, devalues their past experience and belittles those who are not academically inclined.

All Christians need to learn, not just those who have the time and the aptitude for a three-year Readers' or Local Preachers' or Deacons' course. Otherwise we return to a hierarchy where knowledge is power and we try to rely on a dwindling number of clergy and the semi-clericalised to train the rest of the Church. We need to go back to our roots.

New Testament training

Jesus was popularly called 'Rabbi'[1] because he taught like the Jewish rabbis. They in turn, though many would have rejected the idea with horror, had copied some of their methods from the Greek philosophers. Early church leaders imitated many of the methods of Christ and so unwittingly founded their approach on those of Socrates and Aristotle. We can identify certain characteristics of the philosophers/rabbis/early church leaders:

(a) They lived in a community. Plato was surrounded by his followers. When the followers of John switched allegiance to Jesus, they moved from one group of disciples to another (John 1:35–9). The normal missionary team was 'Paul and his companions' (Acts 13:13).

(b) As a result the teaching was in a group: sometimes they walked along together or they sat and talked.

(c) Disciples copied their rabbis. Some even tried to find out the most intimate details of their rabbi's personal toilet so that they could imitate him, just as the followers of Plato copied his stoop.[2] This explains why Paul says,

'Be imitators of me', which to our ears sounds exceedingly arrogant but would be a normal injunction from a
teacher of the period.[3]

(d) Teaching was usually by question and answer – and
even a twelve-year-old boy was allowed to take part.[4]

It sounds much more like a house or nurture group than the lectures or sermons that we so often rely upon for instruction in the
Church. It certainly accords with what we know of Jesus' way of
teaching – the fellowship of disciples and the teaching of a group,
often by dialogue and by the *imitatio Christi*. Even in such details
as the walking and talking, and the sitting and discussing, and in
responding to questions he was following the rabbinic pattern.

Apprentices and students

The rabbis were using what is sometimes called the 'apprenticeship model'. The master craftsman instructs a group of newcomers to the trade. They stand around him as he demonstrates,
and then he says to each in turn, 'Now you have a go'. It is personally uncomfortable as the master shakes his head over some
clumsiness while the rest mock uneasily, knowing that it will soon
be their turn. It is repetitive: the apprentice tries again and again
until he gets it right, so it a slow way to learn – but it is thorough.
One bricklayer said to me with pride, 'It's forty years since I left
the trade, but I can still lay a straight line of bricks.'

I contrasted that bricklayer's expertise with my own virtually
non-existent memory of the French and maths and geography I
had learnt at school fifty years ago. Hardly anything remains. As
a student I learned fast, but also forgot fast because I learnt
superficially in order to pass an exam. Lacking reinforcement the
facts were soon forgotten. After three months those taught as students retain only 10 per cent of what they have learned; those who
use apprenticeship methods retain 65 per cent.[5] Apprentices learn
in a group: students learn by themselves in such intensely individualistic places as libraries and lecture halls – and regurgitate
their knowledge in that loneliest place of all: an exam room.

Clergy have been through tertiary education and have therefore been trained through the student rather than the apprenticeship model. It is only after they leave their training course that they become Probationers (in Methodism) or curates (in Anglicanism), and they start learning as an apprentice to a more experienced person. Some denominations do not even have that period of learning.

Much of our difficulty flows from the fact that the practical is often seen as less academically respectable than the theoretical, and therefore it is thought that if Christians are to have the best training possible the academic model is to be preferred. Edward de Bono, the authority on lateral thinking and much else, does not disparage scholarship but wishes that the master craftsman were on a par with the professor:

> There is a place for academic intellectualising and passive scholarship (which consists of repeating what others have repeated about still others) but that is only a small part of thinking — but valuable nevertheless. Broad, practical, robust and action-directed thinking is not an inferior sort of thinking but in many ways superior.

Educationalists distinguish between 'separate knowers' who are analytical, doubting and try to be objective by excluding emotion, and 'connected knowers' who learn from the experience of themselves and others, and will assume something is true unless proven otherwise. The former value individualistic study, the latter interaction with others. However, the ideal is neither of these but rather 'constructive knowing' which combines both separate and connected knowing and 'integrates the inner and the outer voices, the objective and the personal . . . the knower is an important part of what is known and cannot be separated from the knowing'.[6] It is this sort of integrated constructive knowing which Christians should strive for.

At a time when there is a longing to professionalise learning by awarding diplomas and degrees to confirm that we have passed this or the other course, the Church must be counter-cultural. To learn about God and his ways is something which all Christians should be longing for, whether or not they get an earthly award. So often all that is offered is a theoretical, intellectual 'student' model which encourages participants to look for pieces of paper. Apprenticeship teaching which is practical and earthed looks for reward in the satisfaction of a job well done: after all we may not get prizes for being able to make good relationships with other people but it is a gift worth many certificates. There should certainly be a place within the Church so that some may study academically, but this should be the exception rather than the norm. In other words, most of the training in the Church, whether it is in a group, in a sermon or in personal spiritual guidance should veer towards constructive knowing.

It is important that mature lay Christians are given the authority and the tools to help others. The dwindling number of clergy cannot do all the training. It may be true that those who have not been formally trained cannot answer all the questions they are asked, but, in a post-modern age, that is an advantage. Thomas Hawkins says we live in a 'pre-figurative age' where people are willing to live with unanswered questions. The 'post-figurative age' is over, when those with authority had the answers which they needed to communicate. The agenda is firmly in the hands of the taught rather than the teacher.[7] We have already begun: in church after church lay people are leading house groups and nurture groups and being thrilled by the experience. Once again we have to recognise what God has already started.

Holiness

What is a saint?

Many saints suffered painful deaths. Later the Church canonises them and says they are models of sanctity to be copied by the rest of us. If any of them are looking down from heaven, I suspect many protest vehemently that they are being martyred again: 'I was not like that at all' they shout as hagiography after hagiography spills from the pious press.

The world wants real saints. I rejoice when I hear that St Bernadette 'pursued canonisation as other girls pursue a hockey blue', that Mother Teresa was not the easiest of people to live with, and that St Teresa frequently got angry with God.[8] The whole point is that they were ordinary people who handed over their personalities and lives to God, and so he was able to do great things through them, *despite their weaknesses, and sometimes because of them.* Like the Virgin Mary at the Annunciation they experienced the mix of amazement, excitement and fear which is also our reaction as God works in us and through us. We demean them by claiming they were flawless.

What does modern saintliness look like?

In *The Postmodern God*, Graham Ward sees the Internet as more than just something that people surf for hours. For him it is a parable of modern living:

> The drug of the ever new, instantaneous access to a vast sea of endless desire which circulates globally; browsing through hours without commitment on any theme imaginable; dwelling voyeuristically in one location until the pull of other possibilities reasserts. It is the essentially nomadic lifestyle of the net-surfer; these are the characteristic experiences of living in cyberspace.[9]

He sees modernism as tied to specifics – time, matter, space – while post-modernism is like cyberspace where there are no boundaries and no ethics. Anywhere in the world is nearby and everything is relative. Crackpot is the same as the sane, the vile as accessible as the wholesome, the waste of time as demanding as the useful.

To take the parable further, saintliness means the earthing and control of desire so that the real world is seen beyond the screen. The virtual reality of cyberspace is not reality, and escape into a mirage is not life. Modern holiness has to do with wholeness. In an age of fragmentation, it speaks of unity; in an age of self-fulfilment, it speaks of altruism and in an age without anchorage it speaks of the Other.

Our view of the medieval saint is of someone who in a quiet interiority of spirit communed with God. Our view of the post-modernist saint is someone engaged much in care for others – the Josephine Butler, Mother Teresa sort of figure who drew inspiration and strength from God in order to plunge into the suffering of the world. The post-modernist saint may be someone who is a bridge for others between the real world and the real God: in other words sanctity is mission-shaped. The mission of the modern saints is, by the challenge of their example and their words, to jerk people away from the primrose path of self and unreality to truth and the Being of God.

Our examples are not hard to find. The early saints were missionaries. Paul and Peter and the other New Testament leaders; Patrick, Aidan, and Augustine of Canterbury; Francis and Ignatius: all were passionate evangelists equally at home in the Christian fellowship and in the world outside.

The saint for today does not have to be perfect. Engagement with the world leaves scars, and post-modern people are reassured when they see those flaws. Edith Wyschogrod says, 'In an epoch grown weary not only of its calamities but of its ecstasies, of its collective political fantasies that destroyed millions of lives, and of its chemically induced stupors and joys, the post-modern saint shows the traces of these disasters'.[10]

The 'Wounded Healer' is a popular icon for contemporary society – widows understand the needs of the recently widowed: those who best relate to drug addicts are people who have been there, done that and come out the other side. Vulnerability comes before strength: Jesus died in abject desolation before he could be raised in power.

The post-modern saint is one who knows the world and its degradations and still keeps hold of God. The modern world is unimpressed by those who withdraw from the world into a cocoon of piety.

In the same way today's people are suspicious of those to whom faith comes easily. They prefer to listen to those who argue with God rather than those whose serenity seems to accept things as they are. They relate to the Job who flings accusations at God, and the psalmist who can say:

> But I, O Lord, cry out to you;
> in the morning my prayer comes before you.
> O Lord, why do you cast me off?
> Why do you hide your face from me?
> . . . I am desperate.[11]

Otherworldliness is not fashionable.

Nor is commitment, though in an era of serial relationships and fleeting friendships, to give oneself to a faith for life arouses a grudging admiration. Post-modern saints may have their faults, and they may feel bewildered by God but they follow him doggedly. The disciples often felt confused by the actions and the words of Jesus but they had placed their hope on him and would follow him wherever he led.

Finally, the post-modern saint has the gift of steadiness. The present age is one of fads and fancies. Designer clothes are thrown away, not because they are worn out but because the label is no longer smart. Consumerism invades even the realm of the spirit, when those who are spiritually inclined flit from one nostrum to the next, as do those who pursue the latest diet or indulge in a fashionable alternative medicine. The Christian gift of steadfastness resists the transient. This is not only true of the world outside the Church, for the equivalent of this year's fashion show invades the Church as the new models parade down the catwalk – 'Seeker services are so passé these days!' The Christian saint stays close to his or her God and the reality of the wounded world, and looks for what is serviceable rather than the chic.

Facing the future with hope

> The challenge is not to force everything into the familiar mould. We are going to have to live with diversity.

This quotation from Archbishop Rowan Williams[12] could be put alongside one from Tony Blair, who said in 1995: 'We enjoy a thousand material advantages over any previous generation, yet we suffer a depth of insecurity and spiritual doubt they never knew.'

The Church is being stripped of so much. No longer does it have the power, the money, the prestige that it had. Much has changed and 'fresh expressions of church', as *Mission-shaped Church* likes to call them, are burgeoning in increasing numbers. As ten thousand Emmaus/Alpha groups testify, the gospel is no longer tied to a formula and a gospel which Athenians can understand is being broadcast, and it is one which is not 'with word only'. At the moment it is a case of letting a thousand flowers bloom, and resisting the all-too-common British tendency to be more aware of problems than potentiality.

A Church which is stripped is uncomfortable. The old easy chairs are being disposed of and we are being asked to move out into the world, and finding the atmosphere bracing. David Bosch said, 'Christians find their true identity when they are involved in mission',[13] and we are discovering that to be true.

In this book I have tried to underline width. The broader gospel flows from the width of the being of God, and the less restrictively defined Church is shaped by the whole people of God in the world.

Evangelistic Addresses

These outline addresses are based on the principles discussed in this book and have been used in different situations. Each asks the hearers to respond to that part of the being of God which is being described.

These addresses can be given outside church buildings as well as within them, and to non-Christian audiences as well as church-goers. It is therefore impossible to do more than outline the pattern of each address. Where possible, participation by the hearers should be encouraged: even hecklers can be useful! Each contains:

(a) the Aim of the address – this will always include the purpose of the teaching which is given and also a step of faith which those who hear are invited to take.

(b) teaching about some aspect of the Godhead – this is based on Scripture.

(c) some ideas/incidents/stories which illustrate the theme. This is largely left to the speaker to enlarge and make appropriate to the context.

(d) the Step of Faith, its possible consequences and an 'invitation' which expresses the individual's response. The response to the invitation can be something physical – a movement of the body, lighting a candle, taking a stone from a pile, letting sand drift through the hands. The person concerned should have something to take away with them which will become an icon of their step of faith.

The outline addresses

The possibilities of such addresses are as wide as the multi-faceted character of Almighty God and only a few suggestions are given below. They seek to illustrate:

1. God as Creator	the invitation to worship with thanksgiving
2. The God of Hospitality	the invitation to enjoy his company
3. The God of Mystery	the invitation to explore that mystery.

There is a multitude of other possibilities, e.g.

The God of Service	the invitation to join in his work in a suffering world
The God of Laughter	the invitation to enjoy life in him
The God of Ministry	the invitation to let him work through us to others
The God of Glory	the invitation to let him touch our lives with his glory
The God of Healing	the invitation to let him touch our wounds.

You may also want to explore the ideas surrounding the God of Peace, of Judgement, of Fellowship (the Trinity), of Order (out of Chaos). All are possible themes. Indeed, the more we think of God, the more wondrous and wide ranging does his being appear. John could only end his Gospel, 'There are also many other things that Jesus did: if every one of them were written down, I suppose that the world itself could not contain the books that would be written'!

It is intended that each of the 'invitations' should be an opportunity at the end of the address for those who hear to respond in an appropriate way. This may well be during a time of silent personal prayer but it may well be marked openly.

Three possible outlines are given below.

1. God as Creator

Aim: To convey the creative energy of God, so that we may bow down and worship.

Teaching: Take Psalm 95 as the controlling Scripture. Verses 3–5 portray the diverse wonder of creation and this can be built upon (possibly using visual aids). The planet teeming with life and movement. The creation embraces sub-atomic particles and the Big Bang as well as the more obvious beauty and majesty of the 'mountains . . . sea . . . land'. Illustrate from Genesis 1, Psalm 104, John 1:1–2.

The harshness of the natural world should be mentioned along with the inherent suffering in it, seen supremely in the passion of the innocent Christ, but the emphasis should be on thanksgiving.

The inherent goodness of creation – Genesis 1:31 and the satisfaction of finishing the work of many years – e.g. tapestry, home-made boat.

Illustration: Possibly ask the audience to provide stories of what moves them in the world around. The wonders revealed by the particle accelerators and the Hubble telescope speak to scientific minds, but all are moved by a starry sky or glorious sunset or a child's happiness. Many wonder at the balance of and interdependence of living things.

Invitation: The whole psalm is an invitation to sing . . . to worship . . . to bow down . . . to kneel. The theme lends itself to silent awe before the wonder of creation, and, following the suggestion of the psalm, some physical expression is appropriate. An invitation to kneel as a response would be suitable using Psalm 95 or Philippians 2:10.

The prayer should be a commitment to join our lives with the Life of all things and be remade by our Creator.

2. The God of Hospitality

Aim: To help people to respond to the invitation of the Lord to have a meal together.

Teaching: Take Revelation 3:20 as the controlling Scripture with its conclusion, 'and eat with you and you with me'. Note the three elements: (i) the patient God who knocks, (ii) the need to hear and respond, (iii) the hospitable God. Reference can be made to the 'invitation' parables (the marriage feast in Matthew 22:1–14; the ten virgins in Matthew 25:1–13; behaviour at a feast in Luke 14:7–14 (especially vv. 13, 14, 'nothing in my hand I bring').

Illustrations: An invitation card with RSVP. The millions of pounds in the lottery which are unclaimed because people have not asked. The need physically to go to a football match/opera/film/etc. even if you have a ticket. People unhealed because they could not be bothered to go to the doctor.

Invitation: Revelation 3:20 provides its own picture of response – the need to open the door. People should be given an opportunity to show their response – e.g. by filling in an invitation card and handing it in, in an envelope. At a Eucharist the physical action of receiving communion can be used as a response, using the ancient words: 'Jesus is the Lamb of God who takes away the sin of the world. Blessed are those who are called to his supper . . . Lord, I am not worthy to receive you but only say the word and I shall be healed.'

3. The God of Mystery

Aim: To help people to enter into the voyage into the mystery of the Godhead.

Teaching: Any one of the strange appearances of God to the Old Testament figures, e.g.

(a) Abraham and 'the smoking fire pot' (Gen. 15) – God makes promises
(b) Jacob wrestles with the 'man' (Gen. 32:22–32) – seeking the 'Name': the reality of God
(c) Moses and the burning bush (Exod. 3) – God's call to ministry.

In each case there is the need for human awareness of God

and for response. In the New Testament use those passages which highlight the 'otherness' of Jesus, e.g. the Transfiguration (Matt.17:1–9); Gethsemane (Matt. 26:36–46); the post-resurrection appearances.

An alternative approach is to examine the word 'mystery' in the New Testament which represents a secret which is being revealed, but not yet completely made clear: cf. 1 Corinthians 2:1–5; Ephesians 3:1–13, etc. See the section on *mysterion* in Chapter 2 of this book.

Illustrations: Deuteronomy 29:29, 'The secret things belong to the Lord our God'. The nature of a human personality – the different but same person known to friends . . . to family . . . to him or herself . . . to God 'to whom all hearts are open, all desires known and from whom no secrets are hidden' (CW – Holy Communion). If the human personality is so complex, how much more the being of God? Jesus too shows us the superficial – what he did and said – but underneath the Gospels give glimpses of his divinity.

'There is in God, some say, a deep and dazzling darkness' (Henry Vaughan, 1621–95).

Many computer games create an adventure into a mysterious alternative universe, with both threats and treasures along the way.

Invitation: To enter into the unknown, seeking the being of God and the presence of God. In many ways it is the leap into the dark – Kierkegaard's illustration of swimming in a sea '64,000 fathoms deep'. In biblical terms, 'Launch out into the deep and let down your nets' (Luke 5:4 KJV).

A possible conclusion is a guided meditation ending with an opportunity to take the plunge into the mystery of the Godhead. The refrain from 'Meekness and Majesty' by Graham Kendrick could be used: 'O what a mystery . . . Bow down and worship'.

NOTES

Introduction
1. Epworth Press, 1952.

1: Looking at the Realities
1. In 2002 only four priests were ordained in the whole of France.
2. See for example the statistics in Wade Clark Roof, *Spiritual Marketplace: Baby Boomers and the Remaking of American Religion* (Princeton, 1999).
3. cf. Robin Gill, *Churchgoing and Christian Ethics* (CUP, 1999). This is to be distinguished from Grace Davie's argument in her book *Religion in Britain since 1945: Believing without Belonging* (Blackwell, 1994) who stressed the degree of latent belief in Britain. Both are right: Gill defines 'belief' as something much more specific than Davie. My own research in *Finding Faith Today* (Bible Society, 1992) and *Stories of Faith* (Bible Society, 1995) certainly reinforces Gill's position.
4. In the Hugh Price Hughes Memorial Lecture in 2002.
5. Proverbs 9:10.
6. In case it is thought that such endless discussions are peculiar to church members, listen to any group of teachers discussing, 'What do you mean by teaching?' or health workers debating, 'What is health?' These discussions are not pointless – the eventual definition which is hammered out may be of little significance – it is the *process* of debate which is important.
7. William Abraham, *The Logic of Evangelism* (Eerdmans, 1989), p. 95.
8. Michael Green, *Evangelism through the Local Church* (Hodder & Stoughton, 1990).
9. Working Party of the House of Bishops, *Good News People – Recognizing Diocesan Evangelists* (Church House Publishing, 1999), p. 48. It goes on to detail the misconceptions which are common among church people about evangelists – they are all evangelical, footloose individualists who do nothing but preach and intrude on people's lives.
10. Ephesians 5:27.
11. In *Une Eglise pour Aujourd'hui* (Editions Farel, 2001).
12. Peter Berger, *A Far Glory: the Quest for Faith in an Age of Credulity* (Free Press, 1992).
13. From one of the innumerable web sites on the subject.

14. From an interview with *Newsweek* magazine, quoted by Michael Moynagh in *Changing World, Changing Church* (Monarch, 2001).
15. The interaction between religion and politics is examined in detail by Steve Bruce in *Politics and Religion* (Polity Press, 2003).
16. 'Sanctorum Communio – A Dogmatic Enquiry into the Sociology of the Church' (1927), pp. 174, 97.
17. *Radical Theology and the Death of God* (1966).
18. Ninian Smart, *The Religious Experience of Mankind* (Scribner), p. 16. Others have suggested additions: e.g. aesthetics, social involvement, a person or thing which is seen as the means of revelation.

2: 'Not In Word Only . . .'

1. From *Stories of Faith* which are personal testimonies taken from research on people coming to faith (Bible Society, 1995), p. 30.
2. L.R. Rambo, *Understanding Religious Conversion* (Yale University, 1995). In this chapter we look at conversion to the Christian faith. Other faiths, of course, also experience conversions.
3. G.W. Allport, 'The Religious Context of Prejudice', in *The Scientific Study of Religions* 5 (1966). Beverley Gaventa has an alternative threefold classification based on the person's relationship to their past. For her 'conversion' corresponds to Allport's intrinsic faith which tends to see the person's past in negative terms, while she divides extrinsic faith into 'alternation' which is a natural development of someone's past and 'transformation' which is more radical but does not negate the past: cf. B.R. Gaventa, *From Darkness to Light: Aspects of Conversion in the New Testament* (Fortress Press, 1986).
4. cf. Scot McKnight, *Turning to Jesus: the Sociology of Conversion in the Gospels* (Westminster, 2002).
5. Acts 9:17 (my italics); see also 7:58.
6. One of the most important questions from this fascinating passage in Luke 24 is v. 28 where the Stranger 'walked ahead as if he were going on'. If he had not been invited to a meal would he have gone into the distance? Personally, I think so – the two had come to the point when a response had to be made.
7. John P. Bowen, *Evangelism for 'Normal' People: Good News for those looking for a Fresh Approach* (Augsburg Fortress, 2002).
8. John Finney, *Finding Faith Today* (Bible Society, 1992).
9. There are also Methodist as well as Jewish and Muslim state schools, but their number is very small compared with those of the Anglicans and Roman Catholics.
10. To avoid being conned the authorities only gave the reward after the news had been verified! There is also a modern charismatic twist: a prophetic oracle could be called an *evangelion* – but the thanksgiving sacrifice was delayed until the prophecy had been proved to be accurate.
11. In Paul *evangelion* does occasionally refer to the content of the gospel (cf.

Romans 1:2–4), but in the great majority of references it refers to the act of proclamation.

12. John Stott, *Christian Mission in the Modern World* (Falcon, 1975), p. 35.
13. This eschatological motivation is examined further in Chapter 9.
14. The American author Donald McCullough (in *The Trivialization of God: the Dangerous Illusion of a Manageable Deity*, NavPress, 1995, p. 23) comments acidly on this phrase: 'I assume this imagery comes from Revelation 3:20 (I am standing at the door knocking . . .). But why on the basis of one verse has an entire theology and language of "personal acceptance" of Jesus swamped the far more pervasive apostolic call to confess "Jesus is Lord"? The reason, I submit, is that it fits more comfortably with our American sensibilities. So long as I invite Jesus into my heart I'm still in control of things and my personal freedom is in no way threatened.'
15. As defined in *Salvation to the End of the Earth – New Studies in Biblical Theology* by Peter Andreas and Brien Kostenberger (IVP, 2001), p. 167.
16. Jurgen Moltmann, *The Church in the Power of the Spirit* (SCM, 1977), p. 203.
17. cf. 1 Corinthians 2:7; 1 Corinthians 15:51; Colossians 1:27; Romans 16:25; Matthew 13:11.
18. Graham Tomlin, *The Provocative Church* (SPCK, 2002), p. 161.
19. H. Schilling, quoted in David Bosch, *Transforming Mission* (Orbis, 1991), p. 355.
20. William J. Abraham, *The Logic of Renewal* (SPCK, 2003), p. 34.
21. SCM Press, 1952.
22. Walter Klaiber, *Call and Response* (Abingdon Press, 1997), p. 161.

3: What *Do* They Believe? Modernism and Post-modernism

1. Inevitably writers have tried to improve on the word 'post-modernism'. Some suggest 'late-modernity', 'hyper-modernity' and even 'terminal-modernity'! None seems to have ousted the term 'post-modernity'.
2. It should be pointed out that the claim of post-modernism to have exorcised all 'metanarratives' is itself an attempt to explain all things: i.e. a metanarrative. It is a circular argument.
3. L. Sweet, *Post-modern Pilgrims* (Broadman and Holman, 2000).
4. Monarch, 2001.
5. James 1:8.
6. Z. Bauman, *Liquid Modernity* (Polity Press, 2000).
7. It has been argued that the extraordinary reactions to these events were the 'work of the media'. There is no doubt that the media swelled the chorus once it had started, but those in the media world were astonished by the public reaction and only boosted it once it had started. They jumped on the bandwagon – they did not set it rolling.
8. In Greek *dipsychos* refers not so much to a mind which is divided as a life which is separated into two compartments as can be seen in the references in James.

9. Margaret M. Poloma, *Mysticism and Identity Formation in Social Context (Identity and Character Conference)* (University of Akron, 1997), p. 2.
10. Published by Peter Smith (Latest edition: Penguin, 1991).
11. Peter Jarvis, *Learning in Later Life* (Kegan Paul, 2001), p. 117.
12. See his books *Beyond Decline: a Challenge to the Churches* (1989); *The Myth of the Empty Church* (1993); *A Vision for Growth: Why your Church does not have to be a Pelican in the Wilderness* (1994); *The Empty Church Revisited* (Ashgate, 2003). He is a great myth-slayer: see his comments on urbanisation and the effect of leisure activities on churchgoing.
13. From Mathew Arnold's 'Dover Beach'.
14. While organisations dependent upon attendance have declined markedly, equally significant has been the growth of organisations based on issues or interests which do not expect attendance: the National Trust, Greenpeace, the Royal Society for the Protection of Birds, etc. The Harvard sociologist Robert Putnam noted that more people went bowling but fewer joined bowling clubs: he called his book *Bowling Alone*.
15. In *Understanding Leadership* (DLT, 1989) I argued that the Church had been too ready to accept business practice without looking at the theological and human consequences. I also pointed out that the Church was adept at picking up a management fad just as it was going out of fashion in the business world.
16. I am most grateful to William Storrar who sent me his Quincentenary Lecture 'The Decline of the Kirk' given in the University of Aberdeen and published in their *Divinity Alumni Association News* (No. 18) in Autumn 1997. It well shows the penetration of modernist thinking and practice in the Kirk, and, by inference, in many other Churches as well.
17. *ibid.*
18. Essay by Edith Wyschogrod, 'Saintliness and some Aporias of Postmodernism', in *The Postmodern God – a Theological Reader*, ed. Graham Ward (Blackwell, 1997), p. 325.
19. David Hay and Kate Hunt, *Understanding the Spirituality of People who do not go to Church* (University of Nottingham, 2000).
20. Gerald Broccoli, *Vital Spirituality* (out of print).
21. Hart and Hartson, *Beyond God the Father and God the Mother* (1993).
22. The question was voluntary but 93 per cent of people answered it. Cf. *Britain 2001* published by HMSO in 2000.
23. Note that these figures refer to Britain, not just England. It is interesting also to note where people's allegiance lay: 28 per cent described themselves as 'non-religious', but 45 per cent said they were Anglican, 10 per cent Roman Catholic, 4 per cent Presbyterian, 2 per cent non-Trinitarian (Jehovah's Witnesses, etc.), 5 per cent non-Christian religions.
24. Lesslie Newbigin, *Foolishness to the Greeks – the Gospel and Western Culture* (Eerdmanns, 1986).
25. It should be noted that the research was carried out in England. Although the research has not been done, probably similar results would

come from Scotland and Wales. The different religious background of the Irish would almost certainly lead to different results there. Personal experience of Germany, the Netherlands and New Zealand suggests that research there would have similar results to England, while the United States would be different from anywhere else.

26. Mike Booker and Mark Ireland, *Evangelism – Which Way Now?* (Church House Publishing, 2003), p. 173.

27. John Finney, *Finding Faith Today* (Bible Society, 1992), pp. 33, 34. The comment is made: 'the picture of guilt-ridden, self-accusatory people finding psychological release by turning to Christianity is sometimes painted . . . the great majority do not fit this pattern'.

28. Further details of such services are available at www.alternative worship.org; www.emergingchurch.org; www.freshworship.org.

29. It would be an interesting research project to trace the use of the Christingle from its Moravian roots through its adoption by the Children's Society in the 1960s to its widespread use today.

4: An Overview of Evangelism until the 1980s

1. Report to House of Bishops: *Good News People: Recognizing Diocesan Evangelists* (Church House Publishing, 1999).

2. Galatians 2:1ff.

3. *Recovering the Past* (DLT, 1996); see also Ray Simpson, *Exploring Celtic Spirituality* (Hodder & Stoughton, 1995).

4. The Celtic and the Roman missionaries came into conflict in both England and Germany: in both cases the Celts had evangelised first. Boniface complained angrily to the Pope about those who seemed to him to be ill educated and to have different customs regarding baptism, Easter and, above all, their attitude to the papacy and himself as the Pope's representative. Entrepreneurs are not good at working alongside other entrepreneurs.

5. Unitas Fratrum, sometimes called the 'Bohemian Brethren', were the remnant of a pietistic religious movement which began in the late fifteenth century. They suffered considerable persecution from Catholic authorities and scattered into small groups throughout Europe, one of which ended up at Herrnhut.

6. *A History of the Moravian Church* (1909).

7. K.S. Latourette, *History of the Expansion of Christianity*, 7 Vols. (1938–45).

8. Iain Murray, *The Forgotten Spurgeon* (1966).

9. Research shows that 56 per cent of early Methodists became members of the society before they experienced new birth: cf. T. Albin, 'An Empirical Study of Early Methodist Spirituality' in *Wesleyan Theology Today* (1985). The same phenomenon is reported from many churches: 'belonging comes before believing'.

10. For statistics on the Billy Graham campaigns see Richard Peace, *Conversion in the New Testament* (Eerdmanns, 1999), pp. 288–90.

11. The number of these faded flowers can be well seen in the *UK Christian*

Handbook published by Christian Research. The waste of Christian time and money is immense.

12. Michael Ramsey's movement from considerable antipathy to Billy Graham and his methods to friendship and acceptance is well told in Owen Chadwick, *Michael Ramsey: a Life* (SCM, 1998). He kept a photograph of himself and Graham in his study.

13. The Anglican study *The Army and Religion* (1919) showed that, if anything, the war increased vestigial beliefs in God, prayer and the afterlife. What is true is the shock to the chaplains, who were often brought into close contact with ordinary men for the first time, at how little of the faith the men knew. The same is largely true of the Second World War, when only between 1 per cent and 4 per cent felt they had *lost* their faith.

14. There had, of course, been earlier commercial films which made use of biblical themes: Cecil B. de Mille made *The Ten Commandments* in 1923.

15. Malcolm Boyd, *Crisis in Communication* (1957).

16. cf. The research given by Steve Bruce in *Pray TV: Televangelism in America* (Routledge, 1990).

17. cf. also Tony Whittaker 'Web Evangelism Guide' at www.brigada.org/today/articles/webevangelism.html. The www.reJesus.co.uk site was launched with help from the Christian Enquiry Agency and gets over one million hits a year. The most visited part is the daily prayer space, where people can light a virtual candle, read a verse, say a prayer. It is designed for use by non-Christians.

18. Andrew Walker, *Telling the Story: Gospel, Myth and Culture* (SPCK, 1996), p. 119.

19. Novels of the type of *The Present Darkness* have often been at the top of the American best-seller lists.

5: The New Evangelism

1. Gavin Reid, *To Canterbury with Love* (Kingsway, 2002), p. 166.

2. William Abraham, *The Logic of Evangelism* (Eerdmans, 1989), p. 103.

3. Its fourth edition was published by Kingsway in 2001. The authors are Felicity Lawson and John Finney.

4. We may have been right. In 1994 four big campaigns were held in the UK – On Fire, Jesus in Me, Have another Look and Minus to Plus. The results were less than impressive: cf. pp. 50–2 of *Signs of Life* by Robert Warren (Church House Publishing, 1996) for an evaluation.

5. cf. John Finney, *Finding Faith Today* (Bible Society, 1992). The average length of time for a gradual conversion was found to be four years.

6. There would have been 100+ meetings for those seeking baptism. A similar length is still required for young people in the German Evangelical Church (a minimum of ninety hours) and the Reformed churches in Holland (120+ sessions).

7. The *Emmaus* material is produced by Church House Publishing, London.

8. Published 2001.

9. Produced by Rob Frost and distributed by Share Jesus International.

NOTES

10. Privately published 2002. Obtainable from Higher Severalls House, 89 Hermitage Street, Crewkerne TA18 8EX. It collates the research done by himself and others.

11. Available from Christian Research, Vision Building, 4 Footscray Road, Eltham, London SE9 2TZ.

12. These statistics show the impact of the *published* courses. Courses which are produced by local churches for their own use were shown to be considerably more effective: possibly this is because the authors of a course are more energetic in promoting it, and are likely to be creative and self-motivated people!

13. It is noticeable that the latest (2001) edition of *Saints Alive!* now provides two alternative openings to the course. One is a traditional sin/salvation session, while the other starts with human relationships.

14. In the New Testament it is the word used to describe a host of leaders: Timothy, Tychicus, Epaphras and so on.

15. John Clarke researched people entering the life of the church. He distinguished between the 'osmosis church' where people come through the institutional Church, and the 'web church' where people come because of friendships. A good nurture group draws from both strands. Cf. John Clarke, *Evangelism that Really Works* (SPCK, 1995).

16. cf. *The Adult Christian Education Handbook*, edited by K.O. Granger (Baker Books, 1998), especially the essay by Catherine Stonehouse, pp. 104ff. It is sometimes seen as the difference between male and female approaches to subjects, and between right- and left-brain thinking.

17. Jenny Rogers, *Adults Learning* (Open University Press, 2001).

18. Although I have come across one inner-city church which had 80 per cent plus of the congregation in groups, my own experience would suggest that 40 per cent is high and 15 per cent not uncommon. (A common fault of church leaders is to give disproportionate attention to this segment of the congregation and not enough to the rest.)

19. Published by Zondervan (2002), p. 183.

6: Evangelising Athens – Then and Now

1. A phrase used in the Nationwide Initiative in Evangelism of the early 1980s.

2. The other Pauline addresses are controlled by the situation he was in and are not directly evangelistic and intended to persuade people to faith. His address to the elders at Miletus in Acts 20:18–34 is to Christian leaders. Before Felix and then Agrippa he is making an apologia for his life and ministry: Acts 24:10–21 and 26:2–23 – though it is good to see that he is prepared to challenge Agrippa as to his own faith: 26:27f.

3. Walter Klaiber, *Call and Response* (Abingdon Press, 1997), p. 84.

4. Inevitably some scholars have doubted the authenticity of Paul's speech: Dibelius calls it 'a Hellenistic speech with a Christian ending' (*Studies in the Acts of the Apostles*, SCM, 1955). Whatever view of this is taken the fact remains that this speech is greatly different in style, content and aim

from the other speeches in Acts. Whether or not it comes from notes taken at the time, at the very least it shows how the author of Acts thought that Paul would have spoken before the highly educated members of the Areopagus.

5. Literally 'seed-picker' – a slang term for a guttersnipe who picked up scraps in the market.

6. A similar situation occurs in the translation of the very rare word *splanchnizomai* which is frequently used in the Synoptic Gospels to describe the feelings of Christ towards others: Mark 1:41; Luke 7:13, etc. It is sometimes translated 'to have pity' but this is much too weak. It means a deep and intense yearning for the good of those he was with.

7. I. Howard Marshall and David Peterson (eds.), *Witness to the Gospel – The Theology of Acts* (Eerdmanns, 1998), p. 309.

8. Martyn Atkins in the Hugh Price Hughes Lecture 2002.

9. An alternative word is 'epiphany'. These can be the subject of a very rich study in the Bible. In the Old Testament, besides those cited, are Exodus 33:2ff. (Moses); Joshua 5:13ff. (Joshua); 1 Kings 19:4ff. (Elijah); Isaiah 6:1ff. (Isaiah); Daniel 3:19ff. (Shadrach etc.). In the New Testament are the Transfiguration, the appearances after the resurrection, Saul's conversion and the vision of John in Revelation 1:9ff. Such theophanies are always transitory, in contrast to the permanence of the incarnation. Each showed something of the character of God to the people concerned.

10. See Luke 24:13ff.

11. On the early life of Saul of Tarsus see Martin Hengel, *The Pre-Christian Paul* (SCM, 1991).

12. 1 Corinthians 9:19–23.

7: A New Monasticism

1. Church of England's Mission and Public Affairs Council, *Mission-shaped Church* (Church House Publishing, 2004), p. 116.

2. Steven Croft, *Transforming Communities* (DLT, 2002).

3. Peter Rudge, *Ministry and Management: Studies in Ecclesiastical Administration* (Tavistock Publications, 1968). More accessible may be Eddie Gibbs, *Followed or Pushed* (Hodders, 1984) or John Finney, *Understanding Leadership* (DLT, 1989).

4. Research sponsored by the Central North Division of the Salvation Army, *Leadership, Vision and Growing Churches* (Christian Research, 2003), p. 7.

5. John Drane, *The McDonaldization of the Church* (DLT, 2000), p. 156.

6. John 12:49.

7. Mark 10:43.

8. Gilbert Bilezikian, *Community 101* (Zondervan, 1997), p. 35. Bilezikian is the theologian behind the Willowcreek church.

9. Moffatt's translation of Philippians 3:20. *Politeuma* means 'citizenship' or a gathering of strangers in a place who are organised in the same way

they had been familiar with within the country they came from rather than adapting to their current context. Think ex-pats.

10. John Finney, *Recovering the Past* (DLT, 1996), p. 58. In the book I also showed that the Roman monks under Augustine had a far better publicity machine in the superb historian Bede, and it is his reading of contemporary history which has largely become the received wisdom concerning the conversion of England.

11. On the Continent, where fewer local churches have been changed by spiritual renewal, small communities are more in evidence. A useful introduction to them is *Christian Renewal in Europe* by Graham Dow (Grove Books, 1992). An up-to-date study with indications of what the UK can learn would be very useful.

12. Matthew 15:24.

13. In an interview in 2001.

14. Stephen Platten, *Pilgrims* (HarperCollins, 1996).

15. Donald McGavran, *Bridges of God* (Friendship, 1955).

16. Revelation 5:9.

17. *Shapes of the Church to Come: Strategic Issues for the House of Bishops and the Archbishops Council* (2002), paras. 15, 16.

18. Cf. *Larger Churches Report* (research conducted for Springboard by Christian Research). Paper 4 p. 2: 'churches with an ethnic mix did significantly better than all-white churches'.

19. Pete Ward, *Liquid Church* (Paternosters, 2002). The same distinction is made by Ralph Winter between 'modality' and 'sodality'. The first is the cradle-to-grave Christian community, while sodality describes Ward's liquid church: cf. 'The Two Structures of God's Redemptive Mission' in *Missiology*, Vol. 2 (1974).

20. David Bosch, *Transforming Mission* (Orbis, 1992), p. 466.

21. Stephen Platten and Christopher Lewis (eds.), *Flagships of the Spirit* (DLT, 1998).

22. A useful account of the rise of the Mendicant Friars is contained in Chapter 12 of *Medieval Monasticism* by C.H. Lawrence (Longmans, 1984). The quotation is from page 238. It is noteworthy that most of the friars were lay people, and encountered considerable opposition from the clergy. St Francis was not a priest. See also R.B. Brooke, *The Coming of the Friars* (1975).

23. House of Bishops Working Party, *Good News People* (Church House Publishing, 1999), p. 47. This review of the work of evangelists contains many useful ideas for establishing and supporting teams of evangelists. Although an Anglican publication it is valuable for other denominations.

24. More information is available at the St Thomas Crookes web site: (www.sttoms.net). The basic promises are simplicity, purity, accountability. It was launched by the Archbishop of York at a service in April 2003. They pray five times a day, summoned, not by the traditional bells, but by text messages!

25. See further details at www.message.org.uk.
26. No further statistics are given in the booklet *Leadership, Vision and Growing Churches* to substantiate these assertions, and they need to be treated cautiously until more facts are available.
27. My personal cri de coeur on the matter is in 'A Personal Epilogue' on p. 110 of *Finding Faith Today* (Bible Society, 1992).
28. Hugh Price Hughes Lecture 2002.

8: Leading Over the Hurdles

1. Isaiah 40:3–5.
2. Mark 9:42.
3. There is increasing evidence that after the rigours of a working week Saturday is being seen as the day for leisure and Sunday as the day for shopping and preparing for the week to come.
4. Though we need to be careful not to overstress this – see the final, more cheerful, section of this chapter.
5. Recent research showed that only 10 per cent of primary school children go to school unaccompanied.
6. But note that Paul and the other apostles went to synagogue on Saturday.
7. Oliver McTernan in *Violence in God's Name* (DLT, 2004) has estimated that, of the 115 conflicts in the world since 1989, over half have had religion as a factor, and in 29 it was the main factor.
8. But not a new one. A similar reaction was faced by the Church in the seventeenth century. Cf. C. Greene in *Christ and Consumerism*, ed. Craig Bartholomew and Thorsten Moritz (Paternoster, 2002). After the religious wars in Europe 'the ability of the Christian faith to offer a unified worldview and so provide political and social stability for its peoples came to an end . . . so emerged the faith of secular humanism.'
9. William Paley (1743–1805) was the author of *Evidences of Christianity* which was immensely popular in the nineteenth century.
10. The main findings of the survey carried out by the Churches Information for Mission are available in *Faith in Life* (Christian Publicity Organisation, 2002). The full Report is also available for £500!
11. Geoff Kimber, 'The Church in a Mining Community' in *Quadrant* (March 2002) issued by Christian Research.

9: Ritual and Relationship

1. There are other fields which could be explored – buildings, social action, ecological thinking and practice are all possibilities.
2. Alan Kreider, *Evangelism and Worship in PreChristendom* (Grove, 1995), p. 19.
3. The full story of Gregory's association with Origen is given in Michael Green, *Evangelism in the Early Church* (Hodder and Stoughton, 1970), pp. 226–9.
4. Cf. John Finney, *Finding Faith Today* (Bible Society, 1992), p. 43. Pages

43–7 give many quotations from new Christians of the support that others had been on their faith journey (and one or two where Christians had not been helpful).

5. Leviticus 16:20–2 and also 1:4; 3:2.
6. Christingle began in the Moravian Church in 1747 at a Christmas Eve children's service when the bishop taking the service gave each child a candle with a red ribbon tied round it: the elaborations came later. Curiously in its homeland it is unknown, apart from in the Moravian Church.
7. James Ashbrook (ed.), *Body, Brain, and Culture* (University Press of America, 1993), p. 83.
8. Richard Schechner, *Victor Turner's Last Adventure* (PAJ Publication, 1986).
9. Among other things he built the chimneys of his rectory in the shape of buildings he had previously been connected with. He also did his utmost to help the shipwrecked folk whom his parishioners were gleefully plundering.
10. From her paper 'Mysticism and Identity Formation in Social Context: the Case of the Pentecostal-Charismatic Movement' (University of Akron, 1997).
11. Margaret M. Poloma, *Main Street Mystics: The Toronto Blessing and Reviving Pentecostalism* (AltaMira Press, 2003).
12. The best descriptions of these meetings are by those who were there, such as Peter Cartwright's *Autobiography* and Barton Stone's *Autobiography: Voices from Cane Ridge*, now out of print.
13. Edited by Gordon Melton (Gale Research, 1988).
14. Lesslie Newbigin, *Foolishness to the Greeks – the Gospel and Western Culture* (Eerdmanns, 1986), p. 8.
15. David Bosch, *Transforming Mission* (Orbis Books, 1991), p. 504.
16. Matthew 13:33.
17. Walter Brueggemann, *Biblical Perspectives in Evangelism: Living in a Three Storey Universe* (Abingdon, 1993), p. 19.
18. Ephesians 1:10.

10: The Emerging Church
1. Both by the disciples: John 1:38 ('two disciples'), John 1:49 (Nathaniel), Mark 9:5; 11:21 (Peter), Mark 14:25 (Judas), etc., and by others: John 3:2 (Nicodemus), John 4:31 (Woman at the well); John 6:25 ('the crowd'). Even John the Baptist was called 'Rabbi' by his own followers (John 3:26).
2. And a generation of Anglican evangelicals copied the speech hesitation of John Stott!
3. 1 Corinthians 4:16. See also Philippians 3:17; 1 Thessalonians 1:6; 2 Thessalonians 3:7. Today we feel more comfortable when Paul says, 'Be imitators of God' (Eph. 5.1).
4. Luke 2:46.
5. Study done by IBM and the Post Office.

6. From the article 'Learning from Gender Differences' by Catherine Stonehouse in *The Adult Christian Handbook,* ed. James Wilhoit (Baker Books, 1998).
7. Thomas Hawkins, *The Learning Congregation: a new Vision of Leadership* (Westminster, 1997).
8. My favourite is her squawk when she was levitated, 'put me down, Lord, it is not decent'.
9. Graham Ward (ed.), *The Postmodern God: a Theological Reader* (Blackwells, 1977), p. xvi. He describes cyberspace as a 'cultural metaphor'.
10. Edith Wyschogrod in 'Saintliness and some Aporias of Postmodernism', in *ibid.,* p. 353. Her point about post-modernism is also made by the comic-strip character Calvin: 'Happiness isn't good enough for me: I demand euphoria.'
11. Psalm 88:13–15. Cf. also Psalms 74:1; 79:10, etc.
12. Report of Church of England's Mission and Public Affairs Council, *Mission-Shaped Church* (Church House Publishing, 2004), p. vii.
13. David Bosch, *Transforming Mission* (Orbis, 1991), p. 83.

INDEX

evangelism
  addresses 156–60
  community 119–20
  definitions 6–12, 17
  evaluation 70–3
  new 70–88
  overview 53–69
extrinsic faith 18–19

faith 18–19, 25–7, 29, 32, 34
  barriers 126
  commitments 79–80
  conversion 135
  development 62
  finding 89–91, 136–7
  learning 75–6
  mission 54
  nurture groups 73
  obedience 108
  propagation 59
  statistics 49
  types 101
Falwell, Jerry 67
Feng Shui 13
Finney, Charles 60–4, 70
First Awakening 60
focused community 117–19
formulae 10, 62, 98, 145, 155
Forster, E.M. 28
Four Spiritual Laws 63
Francis of Assisi 28, 153
Franciscans 57, 110, 119
Freebury, Charles 79–81
fundamentalism 43
future trends 155

General Synod 115–16
Gill, David 41
Gill, Robin 5

glass doors 114, 127–31
Gnostics 143
gospel 2, 8–12, 21–32, 43, 53
  Athenian 91–8, 135, 145, 155
  content 60, 89, 91, 98
  history 67
  nurture groups 86
  sharing 102
  sin 48, 50
Graham, Billy 27, 61, 65–7, 70–2, 75–6
Greeks 95–6, 100–1, 148
Green, Michael 7
Greenwood, Robin 125
Gregory (friend of Origen) 136, 141
Gregory the Great, Pope 57
Gregory II, Pope 57
Gregory of Nazianzus 31
Gumbel, Nicky 77

Hamilton, William 15
Hanson, Walter 93
Hart and Hartson 45
Harvest Festival 140
Hawker, Robert 140
Hawkins, Thomas 151
Hay, David 45, 47, 121
Heidelberg Catechism 25
Heidelberg Confession 54
heralds 23–4
hierarchy 25, 108, 112, 147–8
Hill, Susan 118–19
holiness 2, 146, 151–4
Holy Spirit 2, 19, 21–3, 28–9
  baptism 57–8, 74–5
  conversion 33
  creativity 140
  entrepreneurs 55–6